ETHICAL *Communication*

ETHICAL
Communication

Moral Stances in Human Dialogue

Edited by
CLIFFORD G. CHRISTIANS
AND JOHN C. MERRILL

University of Missouri Press
Columbia and London

University of Missouri Press
Columbia and London
Copyright © 2009 by
The Curators of the University of Missouri
University of Missouri Press, Columbia, Missouri 65201
Printed and bound in the United States of America
All rights reserved

5   4   3   2   1   13   12   11   10   09

Library of Congress Cataloging-in-Publication Data

Ethical communication : moral stances in human dialogue /
edited by Clifford G. Christians and John C. Merrill.
    p. cm.
  Includes bibliographical references and index.
  Summary: "Communication ethics are approached from five
perspectives--altruistic, egoistic, autonomous, legalist, and
communitarian--in essays examining the thought of major thinkers
ranging from Aristotle to the Dalai Lama. Each profile provides
insight into how important ethical concepts can help the modern
communicator"--Provided by publisher.
  ISBN 978-0-8262-1839-1 (cloth : alk. paper) —
  ISBN 978-0-8262-1846-9 (pbk. : alk. paper)
  1. Conduct of life. 2. Ethics. I. Christians, Clifford G. II. Merrill,
John Calhoun, 1924–
  BJ1521.E84 2009
  175—dc22

                                               2008055784

♾™ This paper meets the requirements of the
American National Standard for Permanence of Paper
for Printed Library Materials, Z39.48, 1984.

Design and Typesetting: Kristie Lee
Printing and Binding: Integrated Book Technology, Inc.
Typefaces: Minion and Eurose Heavyface

The University of Missouri Press gratefully acknowledges the support
of the Missouri School of Journalism in the publication of this book.

Contents

ETHICAL *Communication*

Introduction

**CLIFFORD G. CHRISTIANS
AND JOHN C. MERRILL**

In the postmodern world of shifting norms and displeasure with the idea of objectivity, there is a need for some stable concepts and identifiable stances. Without them, no fruitful dialogue on ethics can occur. In an era when ethical issues are more urgent than ever, the need for such a resource is a pressing one. The editors of this book hope that by presenting such moral perspectives within a five-stance typology, useful schema will emerge for seeking the right actions. Rather than give up on moral thinking in our day, the profiles of moral thinkers within this collection challenge us to take seriously the abundance of good ideas in ethics that the human race provides us. The profiles speak to real life struggles, but have the lasting quality of foundations. Many of the root values to which they appeal are cross-cultural and some are universal.

The five ethical perspectives exemplified on the following pages by two dozen moral mentors should provide seminal ideas for the communicators of today who desire improved discussion and social progress. Ethics has widespread roots that twist and turn around the globe, but all lead (some more directly than others) to the nourishment and preservation of a huge moral tree. What these moral teachers expound for us is diversity of means to the universal ends of personal and social betterment.

We have chosen to look at leaders who represent five different approaches to ethics. The profiles of these moral theorists presented here are superficial, of necessity. They only serve to focus the reader on the basic rudiments of individual ethical perspectives. It is true that in some respects all the ethicists' thinking goes beyond the category in which they are placed. For example, Immanuel Kant is represented under the legal domain, but certainly he can be read to embody elements of egoism and of communitarianism. And even a form of utilitarianism underlies Kant's deontology in that his basic principles or maxims were originally formed by considering consequences. Mills's preoccupation with freedom means that he could be included in Part III. There is a Confucian virtue-emphasis in Aristotle; and in their appeal to reason and self-interest, Ayn Rand and Aristotle have much in common. There are many similarities in the peaceful approaches of the Dalai Lama and Gandhi.

The editors do not want these five categories or stances to be closed or inviolable, but to serve as broad ways of looking at dominant ideas in moral and religious philosophy. For one can be predominantly an altruist and at the same time have egoist proclivities. And one can be, and probably is, a communitarian and an altruist at the same time. The affinities and differences among these thinkers are numerous, and the profile-writers get into many of them. But we believe that the five-stance typology we present here will be useful in giving today's ethicists an engagement with the foundations of morality. Comparison and difference are productive learning tools; organizing individual ideas into general categories provides one framework for making linkages among divergence.

Louis Hodges follows a similar overview of the field, and also classifies ethics into five domains. In his view, valid moral judgments ultimately are based on virtue (Aristotle), love (Jesus), rights (Locke), duty (Kant), or results (Mill). Over the history of ideas, these five are the bases which have been chosen to anchor ethical systems. While each has legitimacy in terms of its own internal rationale, no one alone answers the issues conclusively. Hodges argues for using multiple theories in order to give nuance and complexity to ethical thinking, similar to a triangulation strategy that approaches problems from various angles of vision.

With typologies such as these, one sees the breadth and depth of ethics as a whole, and it challenges us to critique our personal perspective against its alternatives. This introduction to the history of ethics helps us build on the past without repeating it. Many of our struggles today are ongoing problems on the human agenda which we can address more competently when the wisdom of informed others is at hand. Embodying the concepts and issues through real people communicates more effectively than abstractions do, and therefore makes the wealth of ideas in human history more accessible.

While encouraging students and teachers to take ethical theories seriously, putting theories in personal terms overcomes the canonicity problem. The authority of the canon is under attack at present. The classic lists of big-name theorists have been rejected as largely Western, male, and paternalistic. Credible theory must be multicultural, gender inclusive, and transnational instead. *Ethical Communication* meets those standards. Instead of being immobilized by the discrediting of intellectual leadership, this book broadens the range of theories and makes theorizing more dynamic. Instead of freezing an elite set of concepts into a scholastic monopoly, influential ideas inside and outside the academy are brought into dialogue with our readers.

To facilitate this encounter, the profiles accomplish similar tasks. They provide basic biographical data, main themes or major ethical ideas, and potential for use by communicators. Each profile also briefly presents a few of the fundamentals stemming from the profiled person. For example, Mother Teresa's profile includes compassion, selfless service, and sacrifice. And with the Dalai Lama we see some of the same fundamentals plus his emphasis on restraint, universal responsibility, peace, and disarmament. These values seem to be widespread, perhaps even universal, with exceptions such as Machiavelli. They are residuals that sift from the thought of a variety of notable thinkers and thereby challenge us to consider them seriously for ourselves.

No attempt is made here to present specific cases and ethical quandaries in modern life. Plenty of books do that. We believe, as do the ethicists we profile, that language or communication is the starting point and foundation of ethical concern. A consideration of moral ideas attunes the mind to right action. Moral philosophers are not the only ones who want to know what the good life means; human beings themselves work out together what a good life entails. While the theorists here often speculate broadly about the nature and grounds of morality, the ethical self in our lived experience emerges dialogically, and encompasses several related concerns. These include the search for ethical communication patterns that sustain relationships and build communities. Another concern centers on efforts to uncover those dialogical virtues that inspire moral development and the impulse to engage in moral conversations. Linguistic choices are implicitly ethical choices because they help shape those relationships for good or ill.

At the end is action; but in the beginning is the word. In our dialogue, we invigorate our moral awareness and move our communities to higher levels of morality. These profiles enable us to carry from history and the globe conceptions of moral agency that both liberate and empower our value formation. *Ethical Communication,* then, has a great deal to do with establishing an ethical community. In our dialogue we invigorate our moral awareness and move our communities to higher levels of morality. While moral progress is not inevitable over civilizations, moral growth personally and in communities is nevertheless possible.

Normally, the average citizen when thinking about ethics places special emphasis on altruism (Part I of this book). In his stress on humanistic, unselfish morality, the Dalai Lama is a prototypical altruist. For him, much like the Jewish philosopher Martin Buber and the contemporary thinker Emmanuel Levinas, the other person is the source of ethics and one should always base ethical action on what would benefit the other. All the altruists profiled in Part I are concerned for others, personally (Carol Gilligan) or impersonally (John Stuart Mill). In that sense, a distinction can be drawn between an individual and social altruism.

Or in another way to describe Part I, we identify here an ethics centered on others, ranging from Mill's social utilitarianism to the Dalai Lama's supreme human emotion—compassion and the *agape* (caring love) of Jesus. There are other altruists such as Carol Gilligan who represent a mainstream system of humanistic ethics. Martin Luther King, Jr., and Mother Teresa, whose ethical positions are committed to others, have their main source in the teachings of Jesus.

Part I profiles exemplars of the altruistic ethical stance that reflect David Hume's emphasis on sympathy, the core of his morality. Unlike Thomas Hobbes, who believed that all acts of kindness were selfishly motivated, the altruists of Part I are more Humean than Hobbesian. The keywords here are consideration of others, help and caring, treating others fairly. Such an ethics certainly has a pragmatic value for communicators in deciding how to treat different people in their dialogue and transmission of mediated messages.

But this "other-centered" ethics is countered by a more "self-centered" stance. In the modern world it was Nietzsche who challenged traditional ethical thought and enthroned individuals as the center and measure of life, as the creators of values based on themselves. The thought of those profiled in Part II revolves around Nietzsche in this egoistic orbit. The ethical egoist claims that all persons should try to achieve their own best interest. In many ways, Machiavelli was a precursor to Nietzsche in his private versus public insistence that individuals should survive by breaking free of conventional laws whenever necessary.

In Part II, we have an ethical stance that focuses on the self. Since, for Nietzsche, the God of earlier ethical systems such as Judaism and Christianity was dead, the authority for ethics passed to the individual person. The egoistic ethicists profiled in Part II of this book provide the individual, self-enhancement stance that has manifested itself throughout the history of philosophy, but with a distinctive dominance in the West since the Enlightenment. Also in this second stance, we find the ethics of self-realization in Aristotle, the reasoned self-respect of Ayn Rand, the existential ethics of Camus, and the authoritative leadership ethics of Kautilya of India. Because of his self-reliance and individualism, Thoreau also could have been included here. However, Thoreau is not known as an egoist and therefore is listed under the Autonomy Stance instead.

"Be autonomous and use this freedom rationally" is the concept profiled in Part III. For Enlightenment liberal thought, as one stream, is John Locke's freedom as a natural right. Unlike John Stuart Mill's *On Liberty*, Locke saw no need to rationalize freedom by appealing to democratic politics. For him, freedom was simply a right and one that should be spread as much as possible throughout society. Elitists and rulers should be held responsible by the general freedom of citizens and nobody should be above the law. Locke personified the libertarian tradition of the West and the founding leaders of the United States are indebted to him. Henry David Thoreau in America further stressed individualism and the importance of freedom. Like other libertarians, he did not believe in irresponsible freedom or license. But he did insist on personal freedom from what he saw as undue government pressure and laws. Like his friend Emerson, he put great stock in self-reliance.

Dietrich Bonhoeffer sets the stage in Part III for the ethics of autonomy. Certainly a prime example for modern communicators, this courageous German theologian showed a constancy in his political life, refusing to compromise with authoritarians, defying Hitler, and demonstrating a deep ethical concern for his own integrity and for others. For Hannah Arendt ethics also required maximum freedom. In fact, she might be called the leading ethicist of antitotalitarianism in the twentieth century. Her writings forcefully contradict the would-be controllers and tyrants, and her ethics of responsible freedom stands as a guide to communicators around the world today.

Also in Part III is Freire, for whom dialogue was central. Through the dialogic one establishes common understanding; therefore, Freire could have easily been placed in Part V as a communitarian. But autonomy was a basic concept for this Brazilian educator, too. He believed in literacy (education) as a key to emancipation from the oppressor. Ethics for him applied to everyday life, and one meets the demands of the historical moment only when one's ethics gives a voice to the oppressed, enabling them to speak a "true word," as Freire calls it, out of moral awareness from the inside out.

Part IV profiles a sterner form of ethics. In the tradition of loyalty to authority, Moses, who brought down the law to the Israelites from Mt. Sinai, was the first and his influence was pervasive. But the early Greek philosopher Plato is often seen as the first great legalist in the Western world. Certainly his *Republic* reveals his determination to have a highly structured, elite society built on proscriptions. Kant's philosophical profile serves as an eighteenth-century version of the formalist stance. He placed the individual under a personally devised legalistic ethics determined by his categorical imperative. Duty is the key in Kantian ethics, made popular in Europe—duty to moral principles determined by reason alone.

Another example of the legalist ethics of Part IV is that of the Prophet Muhammad, who in the Qur'an and in the Hadith (a collection of deeds and sayings of the Prophet) taught that the Sharia (path) sets forth a natural law created by Allah and tells people how to act. It forms not only an ethical system, but a whole way of life. In cases of disagreement on the Sharia, decisions by the Ulama (a gathering of Muslim scholars) can resolve the problems.

It was not until the seventeenth century in England that an autocrat appeared who put the ruler above the law. Thomas Hobbes believed that the ruler (*Leviathan*) needed absolute power for society to be possible. His was an ethics of loyalty and obedience to the sovereign. This is a version of legalism which argues that being ethical entails loyalty to authority, to rules and laws, and to traditional values in order to stabilize the sociopolitical order.

And finally in Part V, which profiles thinkers who stress communitarianism, is the view that ethical acts are those that support and expand communalism. This is an ethics of the common good, not one of self-interest. Those profiled here express this common (group) concern in different ways: Confucius in family and group loyalty and following rituals; Gandhi in nonviolent group action; Marx in breaking through class differences; Dewey in expanding education, democracy, and a pragmatic group concern; Habermas in knowledgeable, free, and interested dialogue (discourse ethics), and in involving more people in critical decisions; and Levinas in his determination to give priority to others of the community.

For this fifth approach to ethics, the great Chinese thinker Confucius (K'ung Fu-tzu) leads the profiles. Some may feel that he was not actually a communitarian, but rather a kind of virtue ethicist on the order of Aristotle, whose concept of community went little further than the family. And complicating our use of Confucian ethics, it is unclear whether he saw people as basically good or basically evil. Are people prone to right actions naturally, or are they fundamentally inclined to negative and harmful actions? (His two leading disciples, Mencius and Hsuntzu, illustrate these conflicting sides of Confucian thought.) A thinker like Confucius almost defies classification because of an ideological mixture of meritocracy and community concern. While these uncertainties must be taken into account, Confucius was a group thinker and his familial loyalties and aristocratic manners and rituals were designed to "trickle down" into the general Chinese population. At least it would seem that Confucius, because he saw fit to teach and instill common patterns of action, would see the necessity to enforce any natural, inherent ethical tendencies and thus contribute to the communitarian perspective. Also, such figures as Gandhi, Marx, and Dewey, while evidencing many traits of this genre as community-centered thinkers, are still substantially different in their community concerns. And Habermas and Levinas, illustrating consensus formation and emphasizing other people, are distinct subspecies as their profiles show.

The theories profiled here are not considered abstract authorities. Instead, they assist us in thinking more systematically about the major issues we face today. Theories are not ahistorical foundations of knowledge. They are not *ex nihilo*, concepts arising out of nothing. Nor are they abstract theorems. They identify conundrums in existing theories and show us how to start over intellectually. Theories are understood in this book as meaningful portraits of the world, not artificially fixed formulations derived from external events. Theorizing—in our terms—is the power of the imagination to give us an inside perspective on reality. This is contrary to Descartes and the Enlightenment mind where theories exist outside their context and ought to be as cognitively clean as $2 + 2 = 4$.

Theories are credible generalizations about the world, but none is valid for all time and space. Given that understanding of theory, we are pluralists. This does not mean relativism, with every voice deserving access and a hearing. Pluralism suggests instead that there are multiple legitimate perspectives. In our interpretations of the world, some are coherent, intellectually defensible, and consistent from their presuppositions to their conclusions. In pluralist terms, various approaches are distinctive from one another, but in defending their own legitimacy they grant the same possibility to their competitors. Academic pluralism recognizes the complexity of the intellectual landscape, and challenges us to speak authentically out of our own convictions while honoring the same rights in others. In Thomas Kuhn's terms, knowledge is paradigmatic. Our theories are historically conditioned, complicated mixtures of values, scientific evidence, and political struggle. Some are revolutionary in their impact, that is, they challenge the status quo or open new pathways. Pluralism welcomes these diverse, often competing, high-impact claims about the world.

Sometimes the diversity is only like dialects in language. For example, there are five or six inflections in this book on a common commitment to altruism or egoism and the rest. The different theories within each typology respect each other's approach, while holding its own theory in good faith as well. *Ethical Communication* advocates pluralism among the five philosophical stances also—a weighty, normative pluralism in which these different legacies in ethics contest among themselves, but engage each other in teaching and learning. Students, faculty, and professionals in media, law, medicine, and business face a complex world of expanding technologies and social fragmentation. Approaching these theorists in an open spirit of constructive inquiry will provide resources for engaging the urgent moral challenges of today and the future.

The Altruistic Stance
Loyalty to Others

In altruism, ethical action benefits others, rather than focusing on the self or general virtues, or following the law. John Stuart Mill represents an impersonal social altruism, while the others are flesh-and-blood personal in orientation. In the altruistic stance, the core of morality is sympathy—consideration of others, help and caring, empathy, treating people fairly.

For the Dalai Lama, the supreme human emotion for others is compassion and for Jesus, *agape* (love). Mother Teresa and Martin Luther King, Jr., center their commitment to others on the teachings of Jesus. For Carol Gilligan, the caring one is engrossed in the cared for. In John Stuart Mill's version of altruism, ethical action maximizes happiness and minimizes harm.

PART I

1

Tenzin Gyatso, the Dalai Lama
Universal Compassion

JOHN C. MERRILL

At the age of five, Tenzin Gyatso (1935–) was found in the small Tibetan province of Amdo, in the tiny village of Takster, and proclaimed the fourteenth Dalai Lama (Buddhist spiritual leader). He was recognized as the reincarnation of the thirteenth Dalai Lama, his predecessor. At the age of fifteen (in 1950) he was enthroned as head of state. The Dalai Lamas are the reincarnations of Compassion Bodhisattva who are returned to a life of service to the people. The Chinese at the time were beginning to occupy Tibet and, after Tibet finally fell to China in 1959, Tenzin Gyatso fled the country, going to India where he founded the Tibetan government in exile (*Freedom in Exile*, 23–30 passim).

Since the 1960s the Dalai Lama has become ever more active, speaking in many parts of the world, spreading Buddhist thought widely, and publicizing the cause of a free Tibet. His reputation as a man of peace has grown steadily in the West. He has introduced millions to the Buddhist philosophy and has consistently championed the virtues of peace and freedom. In 1989 he received the Nobel Peace Prize. He has been extremely popular wherever he appears, drawing massive crowds in the West when he speaks. In October 2007, in spite of stringent opposition by China, President George Bush presented him with the Congressional Medal of Honor in Washington, D.C.

The Dalai Lama's message has always been one urging understanding and respect among different segments of the population. He stresses the need for universal responsibility, love, compassion, and kindness. In his 1989 Nobel Prize speech (*Les Prix Nobel*) he said that "simple human-to-human relationships" were becoming urgent.

He went on: "Today the world is smaller and more interdependent. One nation's problems can no longer be solved by itself completely." Thus, he said, "without a sense of universal responsibility, our very survival becomes threatened." We must, he insisted, feel for the suffering of others just as we feel for our own.

The Dalai Lama firmly believes that the reason for behaving ethically is to find happiness. His ethics center on compassion, concern, sympathy, forbearance, fortitude, and patience. In his 1999 book, *Ethics for the New Millennium,* he stated a principal belief that "ethical discipline is what facilitates the very qualities which give meaning and value to our existence" and that ethics should "be embraced with enthusiasm and conscious effort."

Every human act, for the Dalai Lama, has a universal dimension. And because of this, ethical discipline, careful discernment, and wholesome conduct are necessary for life to be meaningful and happy. One of the Dalai Lama's basic tenets is a deep concern for others, and he is much troubled by the fact that there is such a division between the rich and the poor in the world. He sees this situation as getting worse and considers it completely immoral. Self-indulgence generally follows wealth, the Dalai Lama believes, and as such an egocentric life is not a moral life. The wealthy have a tremendous opportunity to benefit others, he says, but too often "that opportunity is squandered on self-indulgence."

It would be somewhat of a stretch to believe that the Dalai Lama's ethics would be very useful (as a general philosophy) to the realistic communicator of today who sees more communication as better. The basic concept of a kind of mystical separation from the practical, held by Buddhists, would fly in the face of the modern technological communicator struggling for profits and power. Self-indulgence seems built into communication, especially institutional communication, and the concept of responsibility is largely ignored.

For the Dalai Lama the elimination or reduction of social friction is paramount. For the modern communicator the publicizing of social friction is considered essential. In many ways the Buddhist idea of communication is one of silence not chatter, of meditation not polemics, of harmony not friction, of cooperation not competition, of peace not hostility. Unlike the communicator of today who thinks that messages must be loud and numerous, the Buddhist looks on the calming and subdued whisper as paramount.

A universal sense of responsibility to others is key to the Dalai Lama's thinking—a kind of megacommunitarianism. He speaks of "intercommunity": international cooperation, with the interests of every person and nation being considered important. He also considers peace essential. In all our communication we should seek peace, promote peace, report peaceful efforts, and take strong positions against killing and war. Simply put, these would be the Dalai Lama's communication ethics.

As for his religion, His Holiness (as he is widely referred to) maintains that it is very simple: "My religion is kindness." No need for temples, and no need for a complicated philosophy. All we need is our brain and our heart—they are our temple, and our philosophy is kindness. His Holiness sees all religions as teaching love, compassion, and forgiveness and making those virtues part of our daily lives. Religion's purpose, then, is to teach self-control and the importance of refraining from criticizing or harming others. Self-criticism, however, is also important. Ethics cannot be separated from religion; a person with an ethical awareness is one who has a religious consciousness.

Buddhism, unlike other religious traditions, is not based on the existence of God. Rather it offers practical guidelines for spiritual growth. As exemplified by the Dalai Lama, Buddhists stress living so as to overcome human suffering caused by hatred and greed in a way that leads to insight, happiness, and peace. It is important to Buddhists that all good or ethical actions—*karma*—that one does today will determine the kind of person one becomes tomorrow. Consequences are important, and Buddhists encourage breaking out of the bonds of hatred and ignorance and cultivating gentleness, serenity, and compassion.

The Dalai Lama's ethical philosophy might be said to largely evolve from the following negative admonitions: not destroying life; not being dishonest; and not giving a false impression. In addition, a person should develop four mental states: love of self and others; pity (compassion) for all suffering; joy in the happiness of others; and serenity (freeing oneself from anxiety). This nontheistic ethical system should prove valuable to the communicator, especially considering the emphasis placed on honesty and not giving misleading information. A deep longing for peace and a desire to suffer with others (compassion) would definitely force the communicator into a more liberal demeanor.

An ethical communicator according to these standards would have a basic concern for the good of others. A sense of compassion will undergird his or her messages. Also, there would be a lack of criticism in the communication. A constant self-analysis or insightful criticism would be the norm. The communicator would form messages with restraint and moderation, and would not incite others to anger or violence. Communication would strive to embrace others, to empathize with them, to support them, to inspire them, to calm their anxieties, and to bring them comfort.

This is in itself a big order. In interpersonal communication, perhaps, it is possible. But one wonders if a journalist, for example, can really do the job of news presentation and analysis with such a fundamental ethics. Wouldn't a journalist's story be biased by an attempt to empathize, to evade criticism, or to calm anxieties? Perhaps, but His Holiness would say that the presentation of an objective news story is not as important as maintaining peace and compassion.

Ethics, then, for the Dalai Lama is more important than simply providing a truthful and full message. Consequences, in other words, are more important than the nature of the reporter's message. In this, the Dalai Lama is a teleologist, and would agree with John Stuart Mill that one's communication should bring the greatest happiness to self and to others. The ethical communicator would be happy if others were happy.

"If you want others to be happy, practice compassion," His Holiness advocates. "And if you want to be happy, practice compassion." Compassion, he says, is not a sign of weakness, but a sign of strength, and it is through the showing of compassion, of caring for others, that a person grows and develops into a complete human being. Compassion, for His Holiness, means more than "feeling sorry" for someone else. It implies an action, some outward sign of help for that other person, some manifestation of care and sensitive consideration. But it starts with communication—intrapersonal communication or thinking—based on words of compassion (*Ethics for the New Millennium*, chapter 5).

Actions are very important for Buddhists. In fact, according to Buddhism, a person's actions constitute God or the creator. As we act compassionately, we become (or are) God. As His Holiness says, Buddhism can be looked at as not a religion but "a science of mind."

The main Buddhist ethical guidelines can be stated in these four admonitions:

(1) do not destroy life (having an attitude of loving kindness)
(2) do not indulge in dishonest action (being generous)
(3) do not bear false witness (avoiding lying)
(4) keep the mind clear (so as to be alert to other people's feelings).

A Buddhist should be careful in all expression. For the Dalai Lama, talking (or writing) is an action. It may not be the final or most important action, but it is an action. Therefore the communicator must be most careful in the framing of the message. It must be conceived of as something that, like a missile aimed at a target, can be very destructive. This is where self-restraint and a sense of responsibility becomes increasingly important. This is also where a compassionate attitude is manifested and where possible consequences are considered. Ethical thinking leads to ethical action. And ethical action leads to happiness.

Specifically related to the media of mass communication, the Dalai Lama stressed that they should be committed to a concern for others. The media have great power, he says, and this power confers to them great responsibility. Media should be socially concerned and dedicated to presenting useful information and hope, but unfortunately they are often consumed with trivial, superficial, or often degrading content, presenting a view of the world that is unrealistically negative (*Ethics for the New Millennium*, 180).

Governmental corruption and other wrongdoing needs to be exposed, says His Holiness, but far too few positive acts appear in the media. Too many stories involving crime and sex appear, placing too much emphasis on the shady side of life. Sensationalism and sexploitation denigrates civility and undermines a realistic picture of society. And the constant and widespread concern with the military, police, drug culture, and criminals have an ethically unwholesome effect on the public.

Millions of kind and considerate acts occur each day, but these are barely reported. The media are consumed with stories of the deviants and the millionaires of society, with the politicians and the athletes, with the fancy homes and yachts of the rich and famous, ignoring the middle and lower classes. The media need more self-control and positive direction. In a free country, this can only come about through the individual communicator's determination to reform, to revolutionize mass communication with an ethic of compassion and an emphasis on uplifting news and views.

Peace, as would be expected, is a big issue with the Dalai Lama. In addition to the Nobel Peace Prize he has received numerous peace awards and honorary doctorates for his promotion of peace around the world. Communication, for him, is very important for peaceful relationships. "The need for simple human-to-human relationships is becoming increasingly urgent," he said in his Nobel speech. And he continued:

> One nation's problems can no longer be solved by itself completely. Thus, without a sense of universal responsibility, our very survival becomes threatened. Basically, universal responsibility is feeling for other people's suffering just as we feel our own. It is the realization that even our enemy is entirely motivated by the quest for happiness. We must recognize that all beings want the same thing that we want. This is the way to achieve a true understanding, unfettered by artificial consideration." (http://www.nobelpreis.org/dalai-lama.html).

His Holiness would have communicators give more attention to the people and groups that advocate peace in the world. This could be through transmitting the peace message as widely as possible, by persuading political leaders to champion peace, and to use the ballot to reward those who support peace. Disarmament is a basic tactic of the Dalai Lama's ethics. Militarization is rampant and only by a systematic and sincere disposing of weapons can we ever have assurance of peace. At least this is the view of the Dalai Lama.

In many ways the Dalai Lama's ethics is akin to that of Mohandas Gandhi, the Indian leader who also was a proponent of nonviolence and a believer in expanding human dialogue. He is a believer in concerted activity of a political, but peaceful, nature that is designed to raise the consciousness of citizens and natural leadership to the many inequities and widespread failure of general social progress (*Ocean of Wisdom,* 21–30 passim).

If the Dalai Lama were a newspaper editor or TV anchor, he would find the typical Western style unsuitable for his message of social harmony and pacifism. He would have qualms about using polemics and repetitive persuasive techniques to change society. He would, as he has in his speeches, recommend diplomacy and condemn any form of force or colonialism. And he would support any government policy that did not smack of terrorism itself. Truth, for him, is important, but in many cases—especially national security and social stability—truth may be limited or eliminated. Compassion, he believes, should always trump truth (*Ethics for the New Millennium,* chapter 5).

Among the outstanding communicators of the late twentieth and early twenty-first centuries, the Dalai Lama is one of the most prominent. In accord with Buddhist philosophy, he does not talk much, but his language is clear and to the point. His English is good and he engages audiences with his calm, thoughtful, and caring rhetoric. He is an animated speaker who blends a nimble mind with a spiritual demeanor that captivates the audience. His writings are also seductive. He stands as a great example of the ethical communicator in today's word-ridden world of superficiality.

■   ■   ■

Dalai Lama. 1990. *Freedom in Exile: the Autobiography of the Dalai Lama.* New York: Harper-Collins.

———. 1990. *Ocean of Wisdom: Guidelines for Living.* San Francisco: Harper and Row.

———. 1999. *Ethics for the New Millennium.* New York: Riverhead Press.

Fraegsmytr, Tore, ed. 1990. *Les Prix Nobel 1989* (*The Nobel Prizes 1989*). Stockholm: Nobel Foundation.

2

Jesus
Loving Neighbors

MARY HULST

To write about Jesus is to invite critique. Those who believe he is the Son of God will take issue with the recitation of cold facts, as if he were simply someone who lived long ago and whose teachings remain influential even to this day. To those who believe that he *was* simply someone who lived long ago and whose teachings remain influential to this day, any nod toward his life as salvific or his death as a sacrificial necessity will raise eyebrows if not hackles.

So this piece will attempt to walk between these perspectives. It offers the facts and reviews the teaching while noting that understanding Jesus' teachings differs for those who believe that he was the Son of God.

Jesus was born in Bethlehem, a small village just south of Jerusalem, in the year 4 BCE. (An error in a monk's calendar has his actual birth off by four years; because of this most scholars do not believe that Jesus was born in the year 0.) His parents fled from Bethlehem to Egypt to avoid the wrath of King Herod, a Roman underling who, having heard from astrologers that a new king had been born, threatened death to all boys in Bethlehem who were two years of age or younger.

Jesus' parents, Mary and Joseph, returned to the region after Herod's death and eventually settled in Nazareth, a village west of the Sea of Galilee. It was here that Jesus was trained in the Jewish faith, though little is known about the years of his childhood. It is apparent from his later teaching that he was trained to be a rabbi, and the trajectory hinted at in the Gospels follows the normal route prescribed for rabbis: learn a trade from one's father while also being trained in the Jewish scriptures, become apprenticed to a rabbi, and then launch into a teaching career in one's early thirties.

In the Gospels that tell of his life (Matthew, Mark, Luke, and John), Jesus begins his teaching ministry around the age of thirty-three. But he not only teaches, he also heals people from their diseases and in a few cases raises them from the dead. This draws many people to him, as the Jews of that era were eager for any leader who gave hope of releasing them from the oppression of Rome. Jesus' skills as a master teacher and miracle worker made many wonder if he was going to be their new king.

Jesus, however, did not seem in any way drawn to political leadership, and this was disappointing to many. Jesus instead seemed most concerned with inviting them into "the kingdom of heaven," and declared that in his presence "the kingdom of heaven [had] come near." For three years he traveled throughout the land of Israel, teaching and preaching his ideas about the kingdom of heaven. People flocked to his ministry. This riled some of the other Jewish religious leaders, who (according to the Gospels) were both envious of his ministry and concerned that he would stir up a revolution that would bring the wrath of Rome upon them.

In the end, Jesus did nothing of the sort. During the week of Passover, a Jewish feast commemorating the liberation from Egypt centuries before, Jesus was crucified at the age of thirty-six. He died, and was buried in a tomb outside Jerusalem.

For some, the story ends here. For others, this is when the story really begins. Christians believe that Jesus rose from the dead and appeared to his disciples. The Gospels, in fact, record that Jesus was with his followers for forty days after his resurrection. Then, after commissioning them to go and make more disciples, he ascended into heaven, promising that he would come back someday.

Some may think that Jesus' teachings are helpful and intriguing regardless of what one believes about his death and resurrection. When he teaches people not to worry, for example, or calls them to care for the needy members of society, it is easy to see how those instructions are beneficial regardless of what one may believe about Jesus' divinity. But the core of Jesus' teaching is a message about love, and that love is defined as sacrificial and other-focused, and here is where the death and resurrection of Jesus matter a great deal.

The word translated as "love" in Jesus' teachings is the Greek word *agape* (ah-GAH-pey). *Agape* refers not to sentimentality or emotion or romance, but instead to a choice that involves sacrificing self for the sake of another. It is a love that pours out so that another can be full.

Jesus' most concentrated teaching on *agape* occurs in the Gospel of John. John spends a few chapters chronicling the last week of Jesus' life, including a detailed account of the "last supper," which was a celebration of the Passover supper and which has become in Christian circles the first celebration of the Eucharist. It is at this meal that Jesus' teachings about love are presented: "I give you a new commandment, that you love one another. Just as I have loved you, you also should love one another. By this everyone will know that you are my disciples, if you have love for one another" (John 13:34).

While the Hebrew scriptures asked Jews to "love your neighbor as yourself," Jesus here asks his followers to love others "as I have loved you." Jesus is referring there not only to the model of love he has already given (reaching out to people on the margins of society, for example) but also, most scholars believe, to the love he will show for his followers through his death. John quotes Jesus as also saying on that same evening, "This is my commandment, that you love one another as I have loved you. No one has greater love than this, to lay down one's life for one's friends" (John 15:12–13).

Some may wonder if Jesus' command to love is limited to one's "friends," but the Gospel of John to this point has been clear that for Jesus there is no line between enemies and friends. Likewise, Jesus' disciples are asked to love all, and to love in the agapic sense of pouring oneself out for another, even, as Jesus himself modeled, to the point of death.

It is this idea of self-sacrifice, not only loving others as you would love yourself, but loving them more than you love your own life, that is at the heart of Jesus' command to love. As Timothy Jackson writes, this commandment

> provides a concrete, and finally cruciform, model of moral excellence that is novel. . . . In going to the cross, Jesus sets a pattern that is radically self-sacrificial, a stumbling block to common-sense ideas of prudence. Any strict reciprocity, in which one treats others as one has been treated, is left behind. . . . [Jesus'] own death on the cross, freely accepted, becomes the standard of perfect love.[1]

1. Timothy Jackson, "The Gospel and Christian Ethics," 45–46.

The grounding assumption in this interpretation of Jesus' teachings and death relies on the concept espoused by Jackson, that the death of Jesus was "freely accepted." That is, that he died willingly not only to provide a model of love to his followers but also, as Christians believe, to redeem the world from sin. In this understanding, Jesus' death is not merely the act of a faceless empire against a good and wise teacher, but a sacrificial and redemptive act proffered by that teacher out of love for the sake of those who were lost in sin.

If that language moves present-day disciples of Jesus to fall on their knees in gratitude, it stops nondisciples in their tracks. Words such as "sin" and "redemption" seem dated at best and wrong at worst. The idea of someone willingly going to execution because he believed that in doing so he would save the world appears to be evidence of insanity.

Can one glean anything valuable from Jesus' teachings on love without acquiescing to the idea of his "sacrificial death for sin"?

Of course. Jesus' own life serves as a model of love aside from his death. Again and again in the Gospel narratives Jesus reaches out toward those on the margins of society. In fact, so many "sinners" flocked to him that the religious leaders of the day mocked him. Surrounded by prostitutes, lepers he had healed, and tax collectors who made their living by exploiting others, Jesus modeled *agape* love long before his death. Jesus' life was one that moved toward others and drew them in. Those on the margins were drawn to Jesus because of his agapic love for them. Because of this, his life can be viewed as a model of how to live.

This model of learning from the life of another is a classic example of virtue ethics. Virtue ethics is a field in philosophy that addresses how human beings are to *be* in the world, that is, what kind of values should they hold, strive for, and seek to embody. While the field began in earnest in the work of Aristotle and was picked up in the early church by Thomas Aquinas (who used Jesus as his model), the advent of the Enlightenment put the ideas of virtue ethics on the shelf. Immanuel Kant suggested that morality began with rules, not virtue. John Stuart Mill developed the concept of utilitarianism—doing whatever increases happiness for the greatest number of people. These two areas of inquiry (deontology and utilitarianism) dominated philosophical thought until the twentieth century, when scholars such as Elizabeth Anscombe observed that since there was no longer a common consensus around a lawgiver (e.g. God), it was time to return to a system which focused on human flourishing, rather than on obedience and obligation. Since then, the field of virtue ethics has enjoyed a reemergence.

Virtue ethics in recent decades has therefore focused on the lives of those humans who have flourished, who have made the world a better place and have drawn others into living as they lived. Jesus has long been an object for this area of study, apart from questions about his divinity. One scholar who used the reemergence of the field of virtue ethics to study the life and teachings of Jesus is Gene Outka.

In particular, and most relevant for our purposes, Outka has looked at Jesus' presentation of agapic love. In his work, *Agape: An Ethical Analysis*, he presents the teachings of Jesus on love and then reviews and engages the scholarly work done on the topic.[2] Outka and the philosophers that he represents are helpful in suggesting how the virtue ethics of Jesus can be applied to all people. They tend to base their work less in the biblical record and more in philosophy, so as to open up the discussion about Jesus' life to non-Christian philosophers and reveal new ways in which their work can be applied. This approach necessarily has its limits, as we have already seen how a person's answer to the question of Jesus' divinity does indeed affect how that person will understand his ethics. That being said, however, Jesus' characteristic move toward others and how all human beings can benefit from its imitation is a rich area for philosophical inquiry.

Jesus' idea of moving toward others has been successfully applied to the communication event in the work of Quentin Schultze. In his book, *An Essential Guide to Public Speaking: Serving Your Audience with Faith, Skill, and Virtue*, Schultze draws from the teachings of Jesus among others to call public speakers to serve their audiences. As he writes, "the materials for learning how to speak publicly have become excessively technical, focusing on skill without paying adequate attention to purpose and ethics."[3] Founding his work on the Christian narrative, and in particular the writings of fourth-century Christian rhetorician St. Augustine, Schultze asks his readers to "faithfully serve audiences as neighbors" and become "virtuous speakers."[4]

---

2. Gene Outka, *Agape: An Ethical Analysis*.

3. Quentin J. Schultze, *An Essential Guide to Public Speaking: Serving Your Audience with Faith, Skill, and Virtue*, 9.

4. Ibid., 10.

Even for those who may not agree with the Christian narrative, the work of moving toward one's audience in an effort to serve them provides an interesting and viable alternative to much of the lesser motivations that exist within the field of communication. Too often the motivation for communication is found in the self: I want to prove myself smart, I want to accomplish my goals, I want to persuade you to do something because it will be good for me. The model of Jesus invites us to shift the emphasis to the needs of the other: Imagine journalists who interview others not only in an effort to please their editors, but also in an effort to honor the person they are interviewing and to serve their readers. Imagine advertisers who not only seek to satisfy their clients, but also produce ads that honor those who will read them and avoid all manner of deception, as well as sexism, racism, or ageism.

What is needed on the side of the communicator is selflessness, and this is not an idea that is limited only to those who believe that Jesus was the son of God. Selflessness can enrich the communication experience because it forces the communicator to move toward the recipient of the communication, whether the medium is email, film, or the spoken word. This move opens communicators to a better understanding of their recipients: in order to serve them well, one must know them well.

Seeking to serve one's audience, to put their needs over yours, is a move that not only imitates the model of Jesus but also has the benefit of creating a healthier community. When I place my needs—money, power, acclaim—over yours, I am willing to do whatever it takes to get the communication job done. But when I place your needs over mine, my whole outlook for my communication project changes. I long to meet your needs, and will lay down my own self-interest for the sake of serving you. If you in turn do the same, a relationship is established that is marked by kindness and courtesy and in such a relationship trust flourishes and communication is enhanced.

The life and death of Jesus hold many intriguing possibilities for communicators. For those who believe he was the Son of God, understanding his death as sacrificial and his resurrection as redemptive provide incentive enough to live a life marked by *agape*. And for those who do not believe, Jesus' intentional welcoming of the outsider and his repeated call for others to do the same provides a challenge toward selflessness. In either case, people who traffic in the field of communication studies can only be served by learning how to serve as Jesus himself showed us.

■ ■ ■

The Holy Bible. New Revised Standard Version. 1989. Grand Rapids, Mich.: Zondervan.

Jackson, Timothy P. 2001. "The Gospel and Christian Ethics." In Robin Gill, ed., *The Cambridge Companion to Christian Ethics.* Cambridge, UK: Cambridge University Press.

Outka, Gene. 1972. *Agape: An Ethical Analysis.* New Haven, Conn.: Yale University Press.

Schultze, Quentin J. 2006. *An Essential Guide to Public Speaking: Serving Your Audience with Faith, Skill, and Virtue.* Grand Rapids, Mich.: Baker Academic.

3

John Stuart Mill
Utilitarianism

RAPHAEL COHEN-ALMAGOR

John Stuart Mill was born in London on May 20, 1806. He was the eldest son of James and Harriet Mill, with eight brothers and sisters. James, one of the forefathers of utilitarian theory (together with Jeremy Bentham), invested himself in the education of young John Stuart and taught him at home. When John Stuart was three, he started to study Greek. When he was seven, he studied Latin. John Stuart acquired knowledge in chemistry and logic before he was twelve. In the words of his father to his friend Bentham, he was brought up to be "a successor worthy of both of us" (Mill 1971, xi).

At the age of fifteen, John Stuart read Bentham for the first time and was enchanted by his utilitarian teachings. Benthamism was for Mill not only a philosophy but a creed, a religion, with his father a type of priest figure. From then on he had the objective in life to be a reformer of the world (Mill 1971, 5–13, 40–50, 80). At age seventeen, he founded the Utilitarian Society and began to work for the East India Company as a clerk.

In 1826, when he was twenty, John Stuart experienced a mental crisis (in his words, "a dull state of nerves") (1971, 81), which prompted him to change his worldview. He remained a utilitarian but introduced new content to it: "The creed which accepts as the foundation of morals, Utility, or the Greatest Happiness Principle, holds that actions are right in proportion as they tend to promote happiness, wrong as they tend to produce the reverse of happiness" (1948, 6). Happiness (pleasure and absence of pain) was still the test of all rules of conduct, but this end was only to be attained by not making it the direct end.

Within this same time period, he became acquainted with the poet William Wordsworth. John Stuart began to value spiritualism no less than intellectualism. He recognized the importance of poetry and art as instruments of human culture. He became aware that the excellent education he received from his father lacked any component of compassion. His ambivalence toward his father grew. John Stuart was unable to conclude whether he lost more or gained more from his father's severe method of teaching (1971, 32). In 1830, he met Harriet Taylor, who was married at that time to John Taylor. Harriet soon became a close companion and an influential figure in his life. John Stuart had found a person with whom he could exchange ideas and disclose his inner feelings.

In 1835, he established the *London and Westminster Review,* a journal which aimed to further our understanding of human nature, to comprehend that feelings are at least as valuable as thought, and that poetry is not only on a par with, but the necessary condition of, any true and comprehensive philosophy (1971, xv, 128). In 1843, John Stuart published his second major book, *Principles of Political Economy,* a sensitive study which details his social and economic worldview. In 1849, John Taylor passed away, and in 1851 the long-awaited marriage to Harriet Taylor took place.

In 1856, John Stuart was appointed as examiner of India correspondence for the East India Company. In this role, he was in charge of almost all correspondence with the Indian government, excluding finance, military, and naval issues (1971, 140). In 1858 he retired from his position; Harriet died in the same year. The products of years of thinking together were soon to be published. Indeed, Mill attributed much of the work to her, saying that the writings were "the fusion of two, one of them as preeminently practical in its judgments and perceptions of things present, as it was high and bold in its anticipations for a remote futurity" (1971, 114). According to Mill, Harriet was the only person in the world who was equal to his father "in her strenuous efforts to promote freedom and progress" (1971, 123).

In 1859, John Stuart published his best-known work, *On Liberty.* The same year he also published *Thoughts on Parliamentary Reform* and two volumes of *Dissertations and Discussions.* In 1861, *Considerations on Representative Government* was published, and in 1863 *Utilitarianism.* Between 1865 and 1870, he published seven other writings.

In 1865, John Stuart, who was always involved in politics as a thinker and writer, was elected to parliament—this despite the fact that he described the working classes as "generally liars" and hardly participated in the election campaign (1971, 67–169). He belonged to a liberal group that opposed the Tory government. However, he did not leave a great legacy behind as a parliamentarian. He was a backbencher who, in 1868, failed to be elected for a second term; this despite Gladstone's win over Disraeli. One of the more significant things he accomplished during his term in office was to initiate a petition calling for women suffrage (1971, 65, 179; 1975, 487). Undoubtedly, it was Harriet who brought John Stuart to recognize the need for women's rights. Mill also fought successfully to defeat a bill designed to prevent public meetings in the parks. At that period of time he was elected rector of St. Andrews University.

John Stuart Mill died on May 7, 1873. His *Autobiography* was published posthumously; *Nature, the Utility of Religion and Theism* was published in 1874; and volume 4 of *Dissertations and Discussions* in 1875.

Mill asserted that his ultimate standard on all ethical questions was utility, insisting that it must be utility in the largest sense (1948, 74). In chapter 5 of *Utilitarianism* he attempted to show that justice, like all other social ends, may be subsumed under the heading of utility; that the desire for justice is a desire for utility (1948, 38–60). Like Bentham and his father, John Stuart believed that the right action is the one which the agent believes will lead to the happiest consequences. Mill thought that Bentham failed to recognize some of the most powerful constituents of human nature: conscience, desire of perfection, sense of humor, love of beauty, love of ease (1973, 330–92).

Mill thought that his understanding of the person was thus more complete, and sought to maximize not happiness as such, but the higher happiness, the freedom of people to engage in the rational pursuit of truth. He was working for social happiness through individual happiness. Mill believed that each and every person is the best judge of her affairs and that the happiness of one is intertwined with the happiness of the many. The freer and more active each person is, the more prosperous the state will be.

The primary principles in Mill's theory are the principles of Rationality, Good Government, Liberty, Truth, Individuality, and Progress. Mill regarded them as valid since they have passed, in his opinion, the utilitarian test: All of them are established as principles because of their conduciveness to the Ultimate Principle of Utility. All of them are essentially designed to bring happiness, to enrich the world with good, and to avoid evil. Happiness of mankind is the general principle to which all rules of practice ought to conform, and the test by which they should be tried.

Mill argued that questions about ends are questions that concern desirable things: "The utilitarian doctrine is, that happiness is desirable, and the only thing desirable, as an end; all other things being only desirable as means to that end" (1948, 32). Mill conceded that people desire as ends many things besides happiness, but this posed no difficulty for him because he insisted that, in reality, there was nothing desired except happiness. Thus, he regarded individuality and progress as ends in themselves and did not see them as contradictory to his ultimate appeal to happiness. These are ends which bring about beneficial effects and, therefore, they are also a means to utility.

Mill, an elitist who believed in the power of the masses to bring changes (often by allowing the gifted few to "show them the light") (1973, 470–72), limited the applications of his theory to civilized communities, to advanced democratic countries. He did not believe his principles could be suitable to all societies. Accepting majority rule in "advanced societies," Mill emphasized time and again his resentment of mediocrity, custom, dogmatism, and violence. This was very logical and practical on his part. After all, mediocrity, custom, dogmatism, and violence are the great obstacles for the leadership of the intellectual elite like himself. The role of the intellect is the pursuit of truth. He relished pluralism and rationality, worked to promote individuality, liberty, and equality in society, and believed in education as a tool to promulgate general principles, intellectual power, vocational skills, professional competence, and "the intensest love of truth" (1973, 201).

Mill wished to promote liberty and individuality. His argument for freedom of expression was strictly utilitarian, in terms of the social benefits to be derived from a policy based on liberty and access to truth. Free discussion was conceived as a means for ensuring the triumph of truth, and it also constituted an important safeguard against the abuse of power by rulers. It is a prescription for good government.

According to Mill, the quest for truth is of paramount utility. He welcomed the dialectic of experience to discover truth. Mill feared intellectual stagnation and stressed that when opinion is verified by experience and observation, then we have sufficient ground to argue for holding it to be true. This, of course, does not entail that it is true. One can never be sure that the truth in one's possession is the truth, the whole truth, and nothing but the truth. Truth for Mill does not lie in the realm of the absolute, but in interplay between beliefs and experiences. The result of these views was an avowed commitment to the idea that we can never be sure where the truth lies, hence all our answers must be tentative and the search for truth infinite.

Even those opinions that we are confident are true, such as Newtonian philosophy, must be exposed to scrutiny and doubts (1948, 83). In the same context, Mill wrote: "If all mankind minus one were of one opinion, and only one person were of the contrary opinion, mankind would be no more justified in silencing that one person, than he, if he had the power, would be justified in silencing mankind" (1948, 79).

Does Mill's plea for truth mean that in the name of truth we should allow every opinion, whatever this may be, to be heard? This question may be pressed further, asking whether it means that all paths for discovering the truth should be left open, so as to enable each person to find her truth. Further, it must be asked whether it means that the Truth Principle *is* immune to qualifications, for example, that we should never lie. Surely this was not what Mill had in mind when formulating his principle. Despite his emphasis on truth, its value, and its contribution to well-being, Mill was willing to allow exceptions to his professed principle. Notice the tentativeness of his remarks regarding truth, in support of the virtue of justice: "Even this rule, sacred as it is, admits of possible exceptions, is acknowledged by all moralists; the chief of which is when the withholding of some fact (as of information from a malefactor, or of bad news from a person dangerously ill) would save an individual (especially an individual other than oneself) from great and unmerited evil, and when the withholding can only be effected by denial" (1948, 21).

Bearing this in mind, we can envisage situations in which we may reach the paradoxical conclusion that lying may serve to safeguard the conditions for searching for truth. There can be occasions where we might resort to lying, believing that in so doing we could gain further knowledge. Someone, for instance, might lie in order to carry out investigative reporting or to gain access to confidential information.

Another criticism of the Truth Principle concerns the infallibility argument. In formulating this argument, Mill assumed that all suppression is based on the asserted falseness of the opinion to be suppressed. But this is often not the case, for opinions are more commonly suppressed because their expression is thought to impinge on the interests of some powerful people (that is, public officials, publishers, and business allies). We can plausibly argue that the dissemination of some views, quite possibly true, ought to he banned in some circumstances because of their destructive impact on the public good. Putting restrictions on the freedom of expression does not ultimately involve a claim to infallibility.

According to John Stuart, and his father James, reason and truth are necessary instruments of progress. Like his father, John Stuart believed that when truth and error are allowed to compete freely against one another, truth will eventually prevail. In fact, he may be correct. The problem here is with the assumption of eventuality. How long does it take before we recognize truth over falsehood? What if the price is very high? Do we still condone the competition of ideas in the market, notwithstanding the price we pay? For example, Europe and the world at large recognized that national socialism was wrong and evil, yet the process of coming to grips with and fighting that evil lasted some twenty years. During this tragic chapter in history, much of Europe was destroyed.

In *On Liberty,* John Stuart Mill wrote that opinions lose their immunity when the circumstances under which they are expressed constitute a positive incitement to some mischievous act. Mill was an ardent supporter of tolerance, and in the name of discovering truth he elevated free expression almost to the same level preserved for toleration of thoughts. Yet Mill acknowledged the need to prescribe limits to free expression. He formulated the Harm Principle that is applicable to both action and expression. In essence, Mill allows freedom as long as it does not negate the other's rights. He explained that the only reason for limiting one's freedom is self-defense.

Inciting words constitute speech which is most likely to bring about harm to another person or a group of people. Those words are also called speech-acts, because it is difficult to ascertain where the speech ends and the action begins. The factor of time, between speech and action, is most vital. Following Mill, the subsequent restraining principle may be deduced: *When harmful speech is close to action it may be constrained under the Harm Principle.* In other words, speech that instigates the inflicting of physical harm, either to certain persons or groups, needs to be removed from the protection of the Free Speech Principle.

Free expression and discussion are, indeed, essential to human progress. Communication between humans is necessary for bringing about awareness, for making us understand issues and their impact on others, and for enriching our world. However, Mill's scholarship should be understood in the context of his time. Some of its aspects should be revisited and reconsidered. Thus, Mill wrote that while incitement in some venues should be prohibited, the same opinion should be permitted for expression in the press (Rees 1985). Mill said this because in his time only the elite read the newspapers, and there was no fear that their reading would instigate harmful action.

Nowadays, the situation is very different. The mass media might play a detrimental role in airing incitement. They might generate an atmosphere of incitement. In our era of mass media, this direct link between inciting words to violent action might be blurred, and it might be difficult to establish clear and direct causality.

John Stuart Mill's concept of ethics was closely related to his firm belief in freedom. He was a strict believer in each person bringing the greatest degree of happiness or good to the greatest number. This would be an individual act and in no way a forced action. One is free to act without coercion as long as no harm is brought to another person. Consequences must be considered carefully before acting, and the act chosen must be the best of possible choices designed to bring about the most good. Mill is definitely a prime example of teleological ethics—an ethics of considering consequences, which is notably different from Kant's concept of following a priori maxims or principles, regardless of consequences.

■　■　■

Capaldi, Nicholas. 2004. *John Stuart Mill: A Biography*. Cambridge, UK: Cambridge University Press.

Cohen-Almagor, Raphael. 1997. "Why Tolerate? Reflections on the Millian Truth Principle." *Philosophia* 25, nos. 1–4: 131–52.

Halliday, R. J. 1976. *John Stuart Mill*. London: George Allen and Unwin.

McCloskey, H. J. 1971. *John Stuart Mill: A Critical Study*. London: Macmillan.

Mill, John Stuart. 1948. *Utilitarianism, Liberty, and Representative Government*. Everyman's edition. London: J. M. Dent.

Mill, John Stuart. 1971. *Autobiography.* Jack Stillinger edition. Oxford, UK: Oxford University Press.

Mill, John Stuart. 1973. *Dissertations and Discussions.* Vol. 1. New York: Haskell House Publishers.

Mill, John Stuart. 1975. *Three Essays.* Oxford, UK: Oxford University Press.

Rees, John C. 1985. *John Stuart Mill's* On Liberty. Oxford, UK: Clarendon Press.

Thomas, William. 1985. *Mill.* Oxford, UK: Oxford University Press.

West, Henry R. 2004. *An Introduction to Mill's Utilitarian Ethics.* Cambridge, UK: Cambridge University Press.

4

Carol Gilligan
Ethics of Care

LEE WILKINS

Philosophy was too seldom the work of women. Until Carol Gilligan.

In her early forties Gilligan decided to listen to women who were themselves making an important choice: whether to abort. The twenty-four women Gilligan worked with were in the first trimester of pregnancy. For some, the pregnancy was planned, for others it was not. For at least one woman, the pregnancy was the result of rape. They repeatedly used the words "selfish" and "responsibility" to explain their thinking.

Thus began Gilligan's intellectual journey into what she has sometimes characterized as kitchen-sink philosophy. One woman, listening intently to other women, heard what other scholars also may have heard before but misunderstood: the moral power of sustaining connections, a different way to conceptualize ethical problems. The women Gilligan studied spoke *In a Different Voice,* the 1982 book described by Harvard University Press as the little book "that started a revolution."

Like many revolutions, much of Gilligan's book was mischaracterized at first. Critics claimed that Gilligan asserted the way the women examined ethical questions was primarily the result of their gender. Gilligan had made no such assertion. In addition, Gilligan's sample was small. Questions about generalizability ensued.

So, how does a psychological, empirical study conducted by a middle-aged woman with few credentials in philosophy prompt a philosophical revolution? To some extent, it goes back to intellectual nurture.

Carol Gilligan was born in New York City in 1936. She earned her bachelor's degree in English literature from Swarthmore College in 1958 and a master's degree in clinical psychology from Radcliffe in 1960, at the end of the era when that institution was the equivalent of a "woman's" Harvard because Harvard did not yet admit women. By the time Gilligan was ready to pursue her doctorate in social psychology, Harvard had changed, and Gilligan obtained her degree there in 1964. About two decades later, in 1986, she became the first female tenured full professor in Harvard's Graduate School of Education. With this kind of lived experience, it is at least possible that Gilligan found herself "unlistened to" in the male-dominated academy. Regardless, her credentials as a feminist scholar owe something to her own professional experiences.

While those experiences may have formed her in some ways, there were other, more traditionally intellectual influences. Gilligan began teaching part-time at Harvard about five years after she completed her doctorate. The first faculty member she team-taught with was the distinguished psychologist (and Pulitzer Prize–winning biographer) Erik Erikson. By this time in his career, Erikson had published two important biographies, one of Martin Luther and the other of Mohandas Gandhi. Both of these figures had much to contribute to contemporary understandings of ethics, morality, and politics. In addition, Erikson's seminal work on human intellectual and moral growth, *Childhood and Society*, was published earlier in that same decade. In that book, Erikson outlined stages of human development from childhood to extreme old age. While the book is psychological in orientation, many of the developmental issues Erikson discusses in it, such as development of trust in infancy, include an ethical dimension. Significantly, Erikson applied his insights in that book to real human beings of both genders. The course that he and Gilligan taught focused on the human life cycle, and Gilligan has said since that time she was influenced by Erikson's analysis of crises and turning points in people's lives.

Her next colleague in the classroom was Lawrence Kohlberg, arguably the most influential scholar on human moral development writing at that time. Kohlberg's empirical work, which employed lengthy interviews with Harvard undergraduates (all men in that era) as they moved through the college experience focused on rights and justice. As a stage theorist, Kohlberg believed that people grow morally in separable stages, beginning with an extreme focus on self, moving through a stage of conformity to external rules and forces, and, for the rare few, moving again to a stage where universal principles are internalized and applied. Kohlberg said that people grew ethically when they were exposed to ethical problems that their current stage of thinking would not help them resolve. But, he also believed that most people, for most of their lives, function in the social conformity stage of ethical thinking. Gilligan notes that because of

> Kohlberg's attention to the moral questions that were so alive in American society at that time, I became interested in studying people's responses to actual situations of moral conflict and choice. I started with men who were facing the Vietnam draft, but in 1973, when President Nixon ended the draft and the Supreme Court legalized abortion, I decided to interview women who were pregnant and considering abortion. Thus, I started on a path that would lead to In a Different Voice."
>
> I remember sitting with pregnant women in the year immediately following the Supreme Court ruling that had given women a decisive voice with respect to the abortion decision. I was listening for how they constructed the decision they were making, who was involved, what were the parameters of their thinking about whether to continue or to end their pregnancy. I remember the sound of dissonance, a voice that did not fit into the categories of psychological theory or the terms of the public abortion debate. (Gilligan 2005)

Faced with theory that was profoundly out of joint with her data, Gilligan took a bold step. She built a new theory, one that she believed better explained how the women she studied made their ethical choices. Unlike Kohlberg, Gilligan did not theorize developmental stages her subjects would move through progressively. Some people got stuck; others appeared to start at a relatively high level. And, even though Gilligan studied women, she believed that men, too, could and did reason in the same way. She called it the ethic of care.

Women (and men) thinking in this way began by considering individual survival. In essence, they make a decision that allows them to "look out for number one." In some of her work, Gilligan called this stage "moral nihilism," because those who occupy it have no thought of "should"; their only problem is getting what they want.

Gilligan characterized the second level of ethical thinking as good-ness as self-sacrifice. Here the women (and men) felt a responsibility to give others what they needed, often at the expense of self. In an effort to care for others, and to sustain relationships, these women frequently put themselves last. For example, twenty-five-year-old Denise wanted to have the baby, but her married lover convinced her that such a decision would have disastrous consequences for himself and his wife. Her willingness to have the affair—an all-too-human kind of connection—meant that she was willing to put others first. But, by putting others first, Denise began to question her own moral worth and to feel manipulated by her lover and that relationship. Goodness as self-sacrifice did not adequately solve the problem.

Finally, some of the women moved to what Gilligan called the "responsibility for the consequences of choice" level of thinking. Gilligan noted that the "essence of moral decision is the exercise of choice and the willingness to take responsibility for that choice." In the case of abortion, it meant acknowledging that there was going to be great hurt no matter the choice. These were women (and men) who understood that life's most difficult ethical choices have no easy, comfortable answers. "The criterion for judgment thus shifts from goodness to truth when the morality of action is assessed not on the basis of its appearance in the eyes of others, but in terms of the re-alities of its intention and consequence" (Gilligan 1982, 150). Unlike conventional goodness, the "truth" of this final understanding of care requires that people extend nonviolence to themselves and others. This universal, and in some senses elemental, understanding meant that women had learned to care for themselves and to include them-selves among that group of people whom it is moral not to hurt. As one of her subjects told Gilligan, "I would not be doing myself or the child or the world any kind of favor having this child. I don't need to pay off my imaginary debts to the world through this child, and I don't think that it is right to bring a child into the world and use it for that purpose." Gilligan's analysis here echoes both Gandhi and feminists from the twentieth century.

The ethic of care is distinguished from the ethic of justice in that it focuses on relationships. In fact, relationships themselves, and more generally real, lived experiences rather than intellectual and theoreti-cal constructs, are considered the genesis of philosophical feminist ethics. Justice values equality, fairness, and a kind of logical detach-ment as ethical decisions are made. The ethics of care values loyalty, responsibility, self-sacrifice, and interpersonal involvement. In the ethics of care, examined emotion holds equal sway with intellectual analysis.

Although journalism's relationship to democracy has been defined almost exclusively as one of rights (think the First Amendment) and of equality (think the three branches of government checked by the fourth estate) it is at least as reasonable to consider that journalists need to care about whether and how democracy works to provide themselves and the profession with courage in tough places. Scholarly work such as *Custodians of Conscience* demonstrates that, for investigative reporters, the results of their work matter in an emotional sense. The connection investigative reporters feel to the better workings of democracy is often a visceral one. James W. Carey wrote that reading a newspaper (and he would have added writing one) is a political act. But, that political act is hardly bloodless, for it should matter a great deal to journalists that democracy in its many forms continues to function lest humanity experience what Plato originally described as the declination of the state.

Other scholarly work has documented that journalists and public relations practitioners use the language of care when thinking through difficult ethical decisions. Invading privacy, sticking with a story in the face of opposition, firing a client who wants a public relations practitioner to lie, all involve acts of care and connection to specific people and to ideas. Certainly Gilligan's notions of listening and narrative have much to recommend them, whether it is reporters listening to sources or advertising professionals crafting a campaign.

While the ethic of care can help explain, and provide additional tools, to support journalists, advertising professionals, and public relations practitioners as they make ethical choices, the overall theory itself may help explain the frequently messy mechanisms of professional growth. For example, Howard Gardner and colleagues in their book *Good Work* describe the profession of journalism as "out of alignment" with its internalized ideals. Journalists at the top of the profession describe the debilitating tension between the corporate-owned organization's need to make money in a capitalistic system and the goals of the watchdog role. Here, care is expressed by the journalists' incredibly reluctant conformity with a specific view of capitalistic media management in which journalistic ideals often come last. This is typical of second-level thinking, as Gilligan describes it. The revolution will come when journalists first decide that it is moral for their ideals to be considered as equally important with wealth creation and then take steps to invent organizations with this different ethic.

The work of *In a Different Voice* was the first of three steps on Gilligan's intellectual journey. In the second phase of her career, she and others did a great deal of research on how adolescent girls form their identities (Gilligan et al. 1990). Gilligan and her colleagues found that, between the ages of eleven and thirteen, most young girls give up their own authentic voices about themselves, their aspirations, and the world around them in favor of a view usually created by authority figures who are most often male. Examining how adolescent girls survive this transition and recover some authentic sense of self is ongoing work for Gilligan. In the third stage of her career, she has attempted to link this developmental process to the role that patriarchy plays in the daily workings of democratic government. "The fundamental contradiction between democracy and the continuation of patriarchy is as deep as the contradiction between democracy and slavery," Gilligan wrote in 2001. "The transformation from patriarchy toward a fuller realization of democracy will be one of the most important historical events of the next 50 years." As part of her ongoing efforts in this area, Gilligan—the undergraduate English major—has written an updated version of Hawthorne's *The Scarlet Letter* which has been performed in a variety of venues.

Applying these insights to daily professional work is, on the surface, straightforward. Listening to sources who are seldom touched, speaking for the voiceless, crafting stories or advertising campaigns with a narrative supportive of authentic community—all of these are possible (although difficult) in the contemporary media world. Peel one layer off the onion and the going gets more difficult. How is a competent professional to craft advertising campaigns that invert a gendered power structure that has existed for thousands of years? Would such advertising sell? Is it possible to use sex as an advertising appeal without simultaneously invoking male dominance? What would happen to entertainment programming if men's and women's roles were equalized? Would Tony Soprano survive as a girl? Would we watch *Sex in the City* if it were about young men? Would either show earn the ratings to remain on the air and in syndication? And, what about the social movement third-wave feminism—the one where both men and women can more freely chose to stay at home with their kids while lobbying politically for a variety of reforms, including the institutionalization of nonviolence at all levels of the democratic power system? These questions speak more to how media content is conceptualized and framed then they do to event-centered, daily choices. Yet, they have profound implications for daily content, too. At minimum, Gilligan's work asks that media professionals reconceptualize their roles from providing information (the libertarian approach) to educating the citizens of a democracy (a more European view). Gilligan reminds journalists that it's OK to utilize care in the choices they make and in their profession at large. And, Gilligan's work certainly indicates that doing the ethical thing is a matter of moral growth—a hopeful view considering the problems professionals currently face.

Gilligan is currently a professor at New York University. She and her husband, James Gilligan, M.D., former director for the Center for the Study of Violence at Harvard, have three grown sons.

■ ■ ■

Gilligan, Carol. 1982. *In a Different Voice*. Cambridge, Mass.: Harvard University Press.

———, et al. 1990. *Making Connections*. Cambridge, Mass.: Harvard University Press.

———. 2001. "From White Rats to Robots." *HGSE News: Harvard Graduate School of Education Newsletter* (October 1, 2001). Http://www.gse.harvard.edu/news/features/gilligan. Accessed August 30, 2007.

———. 2005. "From a Different Voice to the Birth of Pleasures: An Intellectual Journey." *North Dakota Law Review*. 81 N. Dak. Rev. 729.

5

Martin Luther King, Jr.
Ethics of Personalism

WILLIAM BABCOCK

Born in 1929, Martin Luther King, Jr., was the foremost leader of the United States' Civil Rights movement in the 1960s. Making use of nonviolence to end segregation of blacks, especially in the American South, he started the Southern Christian Leadership Conference following the Montgomery, Alabama, bus boycott in 1955–1956. Speaking as an impassioned black minister, he organized sit-ins and protest marches against legal segregation, and during the 1963 March on Washington he delivered his famous "I Have a Dream" speech, which led to the passage of the Civil Rights Act in 1964, the same year in which he was awarded the Nobel Peace Prize. Dr. King's march on Selma inspired the Voting Rights Act of 1965. He was assassinated in 1968 by sniper James Earl Ray.

This minister and social activist was primarily impacted, at least early on, by Mohandas Karamchand Gandhi, the Indian liberator, and the southern black evangelical tradition in the United States. As a result, he combined both nonviolent activism and Christian theology in an ethic of social change. An ethic of love combined with a strong reformist mission to form the basis of King's philosophy.

If King were advising media workers on proper ethics, he would emphasize their being dedicated to positively impacting their communities, to struggling for peace, to nonviolent agitation for social good, and to *agape* love. His overall ethical stance would be a very "personal" form of altruism.

He defined love neither as *eros* (romantic love) nor *philos* (brotherly love), but rather as *agape*, a biblical term meaning redemptive, unselfish love.[1] King used the expression "Beloved Community" to indicate the ideal state of mankind as a whole—the apex of social evolution that he envisioned for humanity, the promised land of racial harmony and international solidarity.

Agape, for Dr. King, was the key to this ideal state of humanity. As he understood it, creative and redemptive goodwill for all people was the source and true foundation of all the virtues which constitute moral excellence.[2] King's own odyssey toward the beloved community resulted in a Christo-centric conception of community that stressed the nature and role of society in the actualization of community. Accordingly, the goal of human community was not merely a utopian ideal for King, but rather the very destiny of the human family, and as a result, human community and international cooperation were no longer options, but vital necessities for continued existence on earth.[3]

The higher moral law was one of the four main components of King's social ethics. The second was the principle of reconciliation. Third, he believed that resistance by public officials or private citizens to social justice manifested a deeper evil, and that reforms were incapable in themselves of destroying that evil. And fourth, the final victory over evil lay in the eschatological (or end-of-the-world) future. To King, no ethical principle was more basic to nonviolent ethics than was the concept of redemptive suffering, and he compared nonviolent struggle against racism to the redemptive suffering of the Judeo-Christian tradition. The nonviolent social ethics that constituted the very fabric of his life required both discipline and a willingness to suffer for a good that was higher than that of one's personal safety or comfort.[4]

King's dedication to God and his loyalty to others—especially those of his own subjugated race—largely defined his concept of ethics. This loyalty to others consisted largely of peace and nonviolence, and it is ironic that for King, and for other nonviolence advocates before him, he would lose his life in a violent manner. The impetus

---

1. Thomas R. Peake, *Ethics*, 3.
2. Marvin Sterling, "The Ethical Thought of Martin Luther King," 92.
3. Walter Earl Fluker, "They Looked for a City: A Comparison of the Idea of Community in Howard Thurman and Martin Luther King, Jr.," 49–50.
4. Peake, *Ethics*, 3–4.

for King's personal altruistic stance was his belief in God and the example of Jesus. And he saw his responsibility as taking action, not simply expressing faith.

The idea of God (a theistic conception where God intrudes in the practical world) was central in King's moral reasoning, and was originally shaped by his black religious heritage and developed in his doctoral studies. The concept, nature, and attributes of God often appeared as themes during King's leadership of the Civil Rights movement. For him, God was moral, powerful, able, and loving, and fellowship with God in the struggle for justice was seen as "cosmic companionship."[5]

To King, the ideal society was to be sought by establishing justice, understood as embodying love.[6] For him, God combined a creative synthesis of love and justice, and thus King conceived of love as an essential aspect of both the private and public sectors.[7] By advocating "democratic socialism," King tried to protect the dignity and rights of individuals while at the same time restructuring the economy to eradicate poverty and inequality. His religious nature forced him to such a radical solution. As Franklin notes, "He [King] embodied intellectual eclecticism with an integrity forged through radical Christian activism."[8]

King's religious roots were in the religion of his black slave ancestors, and slaves and free blacks in the New World forged a compact between their African cultural heritage and their need for a spiritual genealogy. This new religion provided sustenance for twentieth-century American blacks oppressed by segregation. Freedom fighters in both the South and North dissented, and out of this tradition of dissent came the determination to resist oppression, as reflected in slave spirituals:

> Go down, Moses
> Go down to Egyptland
> Go tell ol' Pharaoh,
> Let my people go!

5. Thomas J. S. Mikelson, "Cosmic Companionship: The Place of God in the Moral Reasoning of Martin Luther King, Jr.," 1.

6. Preston N. Williams, "An Analysis of the Conception of Love and Its Influence on Justice in the Thought of Martin Luther King, Jr.," 15.

7. Ibid., 29.

8. Robert Michael Franklin, "In Pursuit of a Just Society: Martin Luther King, Jr. and John Rawls," 75.

Many people viewed King as a modern-day Moses, even though he was a religious leader out of the black middle class.[9]

In *On Being a Good Neighbor,* he wrote:

> The Samaritan had the capacity for a *universal altruism.* He had a piercing insight into that which is beyond the eternal accidents of race, religion, and nationality. . . . The Samaritan possessed the capacity for a *dangerous altruism.* He risked his life to save a brother. . . . The Samaritan also possessed *excessive altruism.* With his own hands he bound the wounds of the man and then set him on his own beast. . . . True altruism is more than the capacity to pity; it is the capacity to sympathize. . . . More than ever before, my friends, men of all races and nations are today challenged to be neighborly. . . . No longer can we afford the luxury of passing by on the other side. . . . In our quest to make neighborly love a reality, we have, in addition to the inspiring example of the good Samaritan, the magnanimous life of our Christ to guide us. His altruism was universal, for he thought of all men, even publicans and sinners, as brothers. His altruism was dangerous, for he willingly traveled hazardous roads in a cause he knew was right. His altruism was excessive, for he chose to die on Calvary, history's most magnificent expression of obedience to the unenforceable.[10]

For King, God is not only love itself, but He has the power to finally overcome all forces operating contrary to love. Early on, King was interested in the concept of social freedom. Henry David Thoreau's treatment of the idea of freedom resonated with King, and he also was impressed with Walter Rauschenbusch's work, which provided him with a theological basis for his concern for social freedom and racial justice.[11]

King's dedication to freedom came largely from Greek and the European Enlightenment philosophers—at least some of them. There is some question as to why he revered Plato and Hobbes since they veered toward authoritarianism in their social philosophy. But he was convinced that freedom, both personal and social, was vital

9. James M. Washington, *A Testament of Hope: The Essential Writings and Speeches of Martin Luther King, Jr.,* x.

10. Gary Percesepe, ed., *Introduction to Ethics: Personal and Social Responsibility in a Diverse World,* 107–11.

11. Ervin Smith, *The Ethics of Martin Luther King, Jr.,* 1–3.

to man's well-being. This was enhanced, says Lewis, by his studies of Plato, Aristotle, Rousseau, Hobbes, Bentham, Mill, and Locke.[12] While agreeing with much of Marx's challenge to social justice, King rejected Marxian materialism and disagreed with communism's ethical relativism.[13]

King usually is associated with the philosophy of personalism, where reality is rooted in a personal God as creator and cause, and where humans reflect the reality and personality of God. Adopting personalism on an experiential and rational basis, King concluded that basic to all reality is a personal God who is the foundation of all being. For him, concepts of personal freedom and the objectivity of value were thus affirmed together, and this understanding had far-reaching implications for King's philosophy of social action. For him there was no real distinction between philosophical and theological ideas as such as truth was truth, from whatever source it came. The test for him was whether something jeopardized the concept of personality, divine and human, and to be personal was to reflect goodness and love.[14]

King expected that a personalism-focused ethics would be effective and lead to a better, fairer world, as is seen in his "I Have a Dream" speech, where he said: "I have a dream that one day every valley shall be exalted, and every hill and mountain shall be made low; the rough places will be made plain, and the crooked places will be made straight; and the glory of the Lord shall be revealed, and all flesh shall see it together. This is our hope" (King, "I Have a Dream" speech, Washington, D.C., August 28, 1963).

■   ■   ■

Burrow, Rufus Jr. 2006. *God and Human Dignity: The Personalism, Theology, and Ethics of Martin Luther King, Jr.* Notre Dame, Ind.: University of Notre Dame Press.

Carson, Clayborne, and Kris Shepard, eds. 2006. *A Call to Conscience: The Landmark Speeches of Dr. Martin Luther King, Jr.* New York: Warner Books.

12. David L. Lewis, *King: A Critical Biography,* 25–265.
13. Smith, *Ethics of King,* 4.
14. Ibid., 15–19.

Fluker, Walter Earl. 1990. "They Looked for a City: A Comparison of the Idea of Community in Howard Thurman and Martin Luther King, Jr." *Journal of Religious Ethics* 18, no. 2: 33–55.

Franklin, Robert Michael. 1990. "In Pursuit of a Just Society: Martin Luther King, Jr. and John Rawls." *Journal of Religious Ethics* 18, no. 2: 57–77.

Lewis, David L. 1970. *King: A Critical Biography.* New York: Praeger.

Mikelson, Thomas J. S. 1990. "Cosmic Companionship: The Place of God in the Moral Reasoning of Martin Luther King, Jr." *Journal of Religious Ethics* 18, no. 2: 1–14.

Peake, Thomas R. 1998. *Ethics.* New York: Salem Press.

Percesepe, Gary, ed. 1995. *Introduction to Ethics: Personal and Social Responsibility in a Diverse World.* Englewood Cliffs, N.J.: Prentice Hall.

Smith, Ervin. 1981. *The Ethics of Martin Luther King, Jr.* Lewiston/Queenston: Edwin Mellen Press.

Sterling, Marvin. 1991. "The Ethical Thought of Martin Luther King." *Quest: Philosophical Discussions* 5, no. 1: 80–94.

Washington, James M., ed. 1991. *A Testament of Hope: The Essential Writings and Speeches of Martin Luther King, Jr.* San Francisco: Harper.

Washington, James M., ed. 1992. *I Have a Dream: Writings and Speeches That Changed the World.* San Francisco: Harper.

Williams, Preston N. 1990. "An Analysis of the Conception of Love and Its Influence on Justice in the Thought of Martin Luther King, Jr." *Journal of Religious Ethics* 18, no. 2: 15–31.

6

Mother Teresa
The Ethics of Sacrifice

JANICE HUME

Tireless laborer for the "poorest of the poor," Mother Teresa of Calcutta (1910–1997) was beatified by the Roman Catholic Church in 2003, six years after her death. This placed her on what some have called "the fast track to sainthood." While living, she won the Nobel Peace Prize and international acclaim for her humanitarian work—for showing compassion to some of the most miserable and destitute people in the world. The Missionaries of Charity, an organization she founded in 1950 with a handful of her students, eventually included thousands of nuns and others in more than 120 countries who sought "towns and villages all over the world even amid squalid surroundings the poorest, the abandoned, the sick, the infirm, the leprosy patients, the dying, the desperate, the lost, the outcasts," to care for them and "awaken their response to His [Christ's] great love."[1] As testament to her life's work, a crowd of three hundred thousand people attended her canonization ceremony in Rome when she became, officially, "Blessed Teresa of Calcutta." Yet despite the acclaim, media attention, and success, she herself lived simply. When she died, she owned "a prayer book, a pair of sandals, and a couple of *saris*, the trademark blue and white linen habit of her order."[2]

Mother Teresa was born Agnes Gonxha Bojaxhiu in Skopje, Albania (currently the capital of Macedonia). Inspired by family members, especially her mother, who welcomed and cared for the poor despite her own struggles, Agnes felt called to the religious life and as a teen-

---

1. Anita Price Davis and Marla J. Selvidge, *Women Nobel Peace Prize Winners*, 108.
2. D. Scott, *A Revolution of Love: The Meaning of Mother Teresa*, 7.

ager became a nun. She joined the Loreto order in Dublin, Ireland, and soon began her missionary work teaching in a high school near Calcutta, India, where she was witness to the crushing poverty in surrounding slums. She was a popular teacher, and eventually a school principal. But that was not to be her legacy. In 1946, on a train ride to Darjeeling in the Himalayas, she received another "call of God." As she said: "In quiet, intimate prayer with our Lord, I heard distinctly a call within a call. The message was quite clear: I was to leave the convent and help the poor while living among them. It was an order. I knew where I belonged, but I did not know how to get there" (Mother Teresa 2001, 12). Later, the Missionaries of Charity would commemorate this date, September 10, 1946, as "Inspiration Day."

Sister Teresa left her convent and gained permission to practice her new mission for a year. She began teaching in the slums, without resources and with only faith in divine guidance. When Pope Pius XII recognized her order in 1950, Mother Teresa initiated ten Indian women, former students, who committed themselves to working for their "community of sisters" and the poor. As the order's constitution said: "We are to love each other with an intense love like Jesus loved to the very limit of love on the cross, without being concerned at all about nationality or social standing. Now that we belong to the Society this must be our true home and family."[3]

Mother Teresa and her order created free schools for poor children—the first met under a tree. Fourteen other schools followed within ten years, including one that served children of lepers. The order founded a hospice called Nirmal Hriday, "Pure Heart," to care for the dying, a mobile clinic and permanent dispensary for lepers, and homes for orphans. Yet building permanent institutions was not the highest priority. As Stiehm notes: "The purpose of their order was to give care in the place that it was needed, and not behind walls. Their work was in the streets, and not surprisingly their own lives were exceedingly modest."[4] In 1965, the church gave Mother Teresa permission to take the work of the Missionaries of Charity to other countries. The first was Venezuela, followed by Australia, countries in Europe, the Middle East, and Africa, and then the United States. Her work and sacrifice were noted. She became a sought-after public speaker, frequent subject of news stories and documentaries, and

3. J. H. Stiehm, *Champions for Peace: Women Winners of the Nobel Peace Prize*, 88.
4. Ibid., 89.

winner of national and international awards, including the 1979 Nobel Peace Prize.

Mother Teresa began her Nobel Prize acceptance speech by asking
all listening to recite the Prayer of St. Francis, "Lord make me an
instrument of thy peace." Brenda K. Kuseski, author of a rhetorical
analysis of the speech, notes that this created an immediate connection with the audience, and committed listeners to action. The word
"love," repeated seventy-five times during the address, was the theme
that held the doctrine and anecdotes together. The focus was less on
sympathy for the poor than on sacrifice.[5] As she told those elites in
attendance, "I don't want you to give me from your abundance. I
want that you give me until it hurts." And the work, she said, should
begin at home:

> There is so much suffering, so much hatred, so much misery, and
> we with our prayer, with our sacrifice are beginning at home.
> Love begins at home, and it is not how much we do, but how
> much love we put in the action that we do.

The work and sacrifice should then spread beyond, she said, "the
poor in our own family first, in our country and in the world."[6]

David Scott notes that the Nobel Prize could have given Mother
Teresa significant political clout, yet she remained focused on her
mission. "God, it would seem, delivered her an international bully
pulpit. But she refused to mount it. It is strange, when you think
about it. In an over-exposed, celebrity-obsessed culture, God raised
up a world-famous saint who ducked the limelight and had no ap-
petite for autobiography."[7] Instead, Mother Teresa continued her
work for the poor, and for peace in the world. She ministered to
AIDS, famine, and earthquake victims, and encouraged the leaders
of wealthier nations to remember their impoverished citizens. As
Stiehm writes:

> Mother Teresa has been described as democratic because of her
> interaction and consideration for the poorest and her equally
> direct interaction with the mightiest who sometimes describe
> her as certain, and at other times determined, persistent, perse-

---

5. B. K. Kuseski, *Quarterly Journal of Speech*, 328.
6. K. Spink, *Mother Teresa: A Complete Authorized Biography*, 299–300.
7. Scott, *Revolution of Love*, 45.

vering, ruthless, uncompromising, even ferocious and aggressive when she was seeking resources.[8]

Indeed, she was a successful fund-raiser. "One of the reasons for her success was her generally apolitical and ecumenical approach to her mission and the people to whom she served. People were able to focus on her simplicity, her honesty, and her obvious care for unlucky people," according to Davis and Selvidge. Mother Teresa's health began to fail in 1983. She suffered several heart attacks, and died in 1997, but her mission continued. "At the turn of the century (2001) the Missionaries of Charity were feeding 500,000 families, treating 90,000 leprosy patients, and educating 2,000 children each year in Calcutta alone."[9]

Mother Teresa's writings, her numerous public speeches and letters, provide insight into her ethical philosophy, which remained faithful to what she had been taught as a young Catholic girl in Skopje. "In many ways she was ordinary and unsophisticated," notes Stiehm.[10] But Lucinda Varley writes: "Behind Mother Teresa's simplicity are years of experience and devotion, in a faith and wisdom unsurpassed . . . [She is] respectfully intimate, pragmatic yet perceptive, vulnerable yet strong, down-to-earth yet contemplative and prayerful."[11]

In a letter to the graduating class of 1986 at Notre Dame University, Mother Teresa encouraged:

> Feeding the hungry—not only with food but also with the Word of God,
> Giving drink to the thirsty—not only for water, but for knowledge, peace, truth, justice and love.
> Clothing the naked—not only with clothes but with human dignity.
> Giving shelter to the homeless—not only a shelter made of bricks, but a heart that understands, that covers, that loves.
> Nursing the sick and the dying—not only of the body, but also of the mind and spirit. (Miscamble 2003, 279)

8. Stiehm, *Champions for Peace,* 97.
9. Davis and Selvidge, *Women Nobel Peace Prize Winners,* 110.
10. Stiehm, *Champions for Peace,* 97.
11. L. Varley, "Introduction," xxiv.

In 1971, she wrote:

> I do not agree with the big way of doing things. To us what matters is an individual. To get to love the person, we must come in contact with him. If we wait to get the numbers, then we will be lost in the numbers. And we will never be able to show that love and respect for that person. I believe in person to person; every person is Christ for me, and since there is only one Jesus, that person is only one person in the world for me at that moment. (Mother Teresa 2001, 49)

Mother Teresa never lost sight of the mission she was called to during that 1946 train ride in the Himalayas. She ministered to real people by living among them, respecting their dignity, and answering their needs.

What can modern communicators learn from the philosophy, and in particular the actions, of Mother Teresa? What would the "call" be for journalists? Mother Teresa would likely advise them to begin at home sacrificing for their communities, to speak for the voiceless, and to respect the dignity of all. In this era of conglomeration and convergence, when, sadly, the pressure to increase profit margins often trumps the journalistic aim of service, she would tell journalists to "give until it hurts." And she would aim her message at the individual journalist, as well as the corporation, even if the path for the individual seemed unclear and unmanageable—just as her path was unclear. "I knew where I belonged but not how to get there."

Mother Teresa made her own way, on faith, yet worked within the system. At every step she sought permission from the church, even if resources were not forthcoming. Her first school met under a tree; she and her sisters lived simply, possessing only the barest necessities. "Providence always comes to our help," she wrote. "When the need is immediate, the intervention of providence is also immediate. It is not always a matter of huge amounts, but of what is needed at a given moment" (Mother Teresa 2001, 38). Thus she continued her work despite overwhelming economic, social, and cultural odds. Journalists, too, must find ways to serve their communities, despite very real pressures. Their "communities" should include everyone, not just the affluent or elite, not just the subscribers or viewers, not just those who can buy the products advertised, but also "the poorest, the abandoned." Journalists should, within the constraints of the profession (including the need to serve corporate interests), put their communities first, place service before profits, and do so out of compassion.

While communicators must work within the parameters of the system—which for most would be the media corporation—they should not hide behind institutional walls. Mother Teresa would tell journalists to get out among the people, report the stories important to their needs, and to sacrifice if necessary to do the work—"to give care in the place that it was needed, and not behind walls . . . in the streets." She would tell them to persevere, despite criticism and pressure, and to remember what brought them to the work in the first place. As she told her Missionaries of Charity, "Go to be a cause of joy to your communities" (Mother Teresa 2001, 140). Communicators should support each other in these endeavors, much as did the Missionaries of Charity, by building networks—families—of those who are doing the good work.

In the end, "The Blessed Teresa of Calcutta" was known more for her good works, her actions, than for her philosophy, just as communicators will be known for the quality of their work more than their abstract ethical ideals. She respected the dignity of every human, and she gave much to alleviate the suffering of the "poorest of the poor." She expected others to do the same, to "give until it hurts." She was not without critics or controversy, in particular regarding her outspoken criticism of abortion and her heavy-handed efforts to convert those to whom she ministered. A decade after her death a number of her letters were published indicating that she had undergone crises of faith, "dark nights of the soul." A column in *Newsweek* asked: "So, which is the more striking: that the faithful should bravely confront the fact that one of their heroines all but lost her own faith, or that the Church should have gone on deploying, as an icon of favorable publicity, a confused old lady whom it knew had for all practical purposes ceased to believe?"[12] James Martin, a Jesuit priest, had a different take on her crisis. Writing in the *New York Times*, he argued: "Mother Teresa's doubt may have contributed to the efficacy of one of the more notable faith-based initiatives of the last century. . . . Her ministry to a doubting modern world may have just begun."[13]

■ ■ ■

12. C. Hitchins, "The Dogmatic Doubter: The Nun's Leading Critic Argues that the Psychic Pain Revealed in a New Book Was a Byproduct of Her Faith," 41.
13. James Martin, "A Saint's Dark Night," A23.

Davis, Anita Price, and Selvidge, Marla J. 2006. *Women Nobel Peace Prize Winners.* Jefferson, N.C.: McFarland and Co.

Hitchens, C. 2007. "The Dogmatic Doubter: The Nun's Leading Critic Argues that the Psychic Pain Revealed in a New Book Was a Byproduct of Her Faith." *Newsweek,* September 10, 2007, 41.

Kuseski, B. K. 1988. "Kenneth Burke's 'Five Dogs' and Mother Teresa's Love." *Quarterly Journal of Speech* 74: 323–33.

Martin, James. 2007. "A Saint's Dark Night." *New York Times,* August 29, 2007, A23.

Miscamble, W. 2003. *Go Forth and Do Good: Memorable Notre Dame Commencement Addresses.* Notre Dame, Ind.: University of Notre Dame Press.

Mother Teresa. 2001. *Essential Writings.* Edited by J. Maalouf. Maryknoll, N.Y.: Orbis Books.

Scott, D. 2005. *A Revolution of Love: The Meaning of Mother Teresa.* Chicago: Loyola Press.

Spink, K. 1997. *Mother Teresa: A Complete Authorized Biography.* New York: Harper Collins Publishers.

Stiehm, J. H. 2006. *Champions for Peace: Women Winners of the Nobel Peace Prize.* Lanham, Md.: Rowman and Littlefield.

Varley, L. "Introduction." 1995. In *A Simple Path,* by Mother Teresa. New York: Ballantine Books.

The Egoistic Stance
Loyalty to Self

In this part of the book we pass from a consideration of other persons to a primary concern for one's self. The egoistic stance may not exclude a social sense, but it stresses development of a virtuous self. This is an emphasis on self-enhancement that has manifested itself throughout human history, though with a greater prominence in the West since the eighteenth-century Enlightenment.

Some ethical egoists claim that everyone should actively seek their own interests. Machiavelli insisted that individuals could best survive by breaking free of conventional laws whenever necessary.

For Nietzsche, since the God of Judeo-Christian ethics is dead, the authority for ethics passed to ourselves.

The more standard versions of the egoistic stance are the self-concerned virtue ethics of Aristotle, the reasoned self-respect of Ayn Rand, the existential ethics of Camus, and the authoritative leadership ethics of Kautilya of India.

PART II

7

Aristotle
Self-Development

LEE ANNE PECK

A person's virtuous character grows from certain habits; this is the cornerstone of Aristotle's ethics. According to Aristotle (384–322 BCE): "It makes no small difference . . . whether we form habits of one kind or another from our very youth; it makes a very great difference, or rather *all* the difference" (1103b25).[1] Some moral theories highlight the end result of a person's action, and others take into account the actions themselves. Aristotle, though, put the emphasis on one's character.

Aristotle, a student of Plato's, believed that ethics is not an exact science; instead, he believed in the uniqueness of individuals and, therefore, that ethical behavior cannot be prescribed precisely. For instance, the virtue of courage sits between two opposite extremes— one of foolhardiness and the other of cowardliness, and the optimal point between these two extremes may be different for different people. What is morally required, so to speak, is determined by the circumstances, or the cultural significance, of a case; therefore, no single right action exists for any ethical situation.

The above description is Aristotle's Doctrine of the Mean. Every virtue lies between two vices: one in the direction of too much emotion, the other in the direction of too little. Some may believe Aristotle's doctrine came from mathematics, but it did not, and it cannot be explained as such. Moral virtues are habits of choice—thus, the study of ethics is action, not just knowledge. Aristotle would say that

---

1. All *Nicomachean Ethics* citations are from R. McKeon, ed., *Introduction to Aristotle* (1947). McKeon used the marginal numbering from Bekker's edition.

what is needed before his mean can be understood and used are "well brought-up beginners" who have the correct virtuous habits.

Aristotle was born in Macedonia, north of ancient Greece, the son of the doctor Nicomachus. In 367 BCE, Aristotle went to Athens and studied at Plato's Academy for twenty years. According to philosopher Diogenes (400–325 BCE), who was an early biographer of sorts, Aristotle was known as the mind of the school, or the *nous*. No evidence of Aristotle exists in Plato's writings; however, evidence of Plato exists in Aristotle's—especially in reference to the Platonic doctrine of the forms. In his writing, Aristotle used no comedy or irony as Plato occasionally did, and he studied such diverse topics as biology and physics.

After Plato died in 347 BCE, Aristotle left Athens for several years, traveling and staying in different areas. It is believed he did many of his biological studies during this time period, mostly on the island of Lesbos. Philip II invited Aristotle to return to Macedonia to teach his son Alexander, who later became Alexander the Great. In 335 BCE, Aristotle returned to Athens and created his own school, the Lyceum; Plato's nephew Speusippus had taken over his uncle's Academy.

Students of the Lyceum were known as peripatetic—they learned while walking and talking. In 323 BCE, when Alexander the Great died, Aristotle's position in Athens became uncertain because he was from Macedonia and not a citizen of Athens, so he left for the island of Euboea, where he died in 322 BCE in his early sixties. Although Aristotle died at a somewhat early age, he left many writings that read like lecture notes (and *are* probably lecture notes). It is believed that only about a third of Aristotle's writings survive today. Aristotle's treatises on ethics include *The Eudemian Ethics*, edited by his student Eudemus, and *The Nicomachean Ethics*, edited by his son Nicomachus. Because *The Nicomachean Ethics* is thought to be the work written closest to his death, many see the views it contains as those most closely mirroring Aristotle's beliefs about ethics.

As mentioned, Aristotle disagreed with Plato's idea of, or form of, the one "good." He believed that the good is different in different actions (1097a15) and only "happiness" is final in all instances. When a person knows the difference between right and wrong, this, he believed, was the state of happiness. Aristotle believed one should enjoy doing the right thing—and practice makes perfect!

According to Aristotle, before a person can put the Doctrine of the Mean into action, a person must *already* be a virtuous person.

He or she becomes a virtuous person via habit; thus, being virtuous becomes second nature. Aristotle wrote: "Neither by nature . . . not contrary to nature do the virtues arise in us; rather we are adapted by nature to receive them, and are made perfect by habit" (1103b23). In other words, morals are not innate. He also said moral excellence involves pleasure and pain. "We ought to have been brought up in a particular way from our very youth, as Plato says, so as both to delight in and to be pained by the things that we ought: for this is the right education" (1104b30).

Aristotle wrote: "Virtuous behavior is to experience emotions at the right time, toward the right objects or people for the right reason in the right manner in accordance with the mean" (1106b20). It should be noted that Aristotle did say some acts were definitely not allowed, such as adultery, theft, and murder. It's never possible to be "right" doing any of these actions; there is no excess or deficiency. For instance, he said that "committing adultery with the right woman at the right time and in the right way . . . is to do wrong" (1007a25). But other than these examples, Aristotle would deny that a simple formula exists to determine how one should act in a certain situation—the answer depends on one's own moral sensibility. With the Doctrine of the Mean, Aristotle addressed someone who wants and enjoys virtuous actions—he was not explaining *why* virtuous actions should be pursued. He said moral acts cannot be set exactly, but he did believe that one's excesses or deficiencies can destroy the virtues. Moderation is a good thing, and action in accordance with a mean will produce virtue. A person must do acts from "a firm and unchangeable character" (1105a30).

For Aristotle, the intellectual virtues can be learned or taught while the moral virtues must be lived. For instance, because of habit, "men [*sic*] become just by performing just acts—just like humans become builders by building" (1103b). The intellectual and moral virtues combine to help us discover what is good or bad; we need both. To live a virtuous life, we must also take into account the rational part of ourselves; Aristotle believed humans are rational animals. By reasoning, we can ascertain what is necessary to live correctly. In other words, virtue is our "end" while practical reasoning or wisdom (*phronesis*) is the means.

Aristotle wrote that practical wisdom cannot be scientific knowledge or art—"not science because that which can be done is capable of being otherwise, not art because action and making are different things; the remaining alternative, then, is that it is a true and reasoned state or capacity to act with regard to the things that are good or bad for man" (1141b1). And excellence in contemplation and deliberation is correctness of thinking. Therefore, much is at stake in our becoming moral human beings, capable of doing ethical decision-making.

So virtue brings us happiness, but Aristotle believed there was a higher state. He was not an atheist; he believed in a god (or gods) titled "the unmoved mover(s)."[2] Explained most thoroughly in Aristotle's *Metaphysics,* his theology needs to be mentioned in the context of Aristotle's ethics. According to Aristotle, all movement needs a mover.

He believed "the first heavens must be eternal." "There is therefore something which moves them. And since what both moves and is moved has an intermediate status, there must be a mover which moves them without being moved, eternal, and a substance and actual" (*Metaphysics,* 1072a21–26). God is infinite and the ultimate unmoved mover, and is separate from sensible things because God has no body. However, God can think, or has thoughts—and the thoughts are divine and unchanging. The unmoved mover moves us but does not move itself, so to speak. Aristotle believed that unconsciously we want to be like the unmoved mover, fulfilling our goal toward the good. If communication practitioners take this idea from Aristotle, they will always strive for the good.

Communication professionals must go beyond memorizing rules when confronted with an ethical dilemma. They must have the excellence of character that comes with practice. Communicators have codes of ethics—intellectual virtues that can be learned or memorized. This is a good place to start for entry-level or student communicators; like children who learn right and wrong, young communicators are taught the basic principles of their chosen professions. However, Aristotle would say this is not enough to know the good: communicators must become good.

Again, understanding the Doctrine of the Mean is not a quick and easy read or lecture. It is not some kind of mathematical equation. If a professional communicator or communications student

2. Aristotle discusses both unmoved movers and the one unmoved mover, God, in his *Metaphysics.* See T. Irwin and S. Fine, trans., *Aristotle: Selections* (Indianapolis: Hackett Publishing, 1995).

is going to choose the correct action, he or she needs considerably more "habituation" than what has been offered to them at work or at school. Aristotle would say that professional communicators and communication students without the proper character-building will be unprepared for the ethical dilemmas they will face. This is not about etiquette; this is about issues of morality. "Elders," such as communications professors, have a place in students' habituation. What one should do is suggested by a more seasoned, ethical professional; this can be a starting point.

Can professional communicators already in the field be habituated? Virtue without wisdom is naive. Aristotle wrote that some people "take refuge in theory and think they are being philosophers and will become good in this way, behaving somewhat like patients who listen attentively to their doctors, but do none of the things they are ordered to do. As the latter will not be made well in body by such a course of treatment, the former will not be made well by such a course of philosophy" (1105b5). Communicators must go beyond memorizing rules and merely listening. They should strive to be like the unmoved mover, strive to think and deliberate, and then act.

The virtuous communicator should meet the following criteria: "In the first place, he must have knowledge (practical wisdom); secondly, he must choose the acts, and choose them for their own sakes, and thirdly, his action must proceed from a firm and unchangeable character" (1105a30). Guidance should come by example from a mentor in a friendly environment, and it should be a continuing enterprise. Too often in the frenzy of deadlines, the atmosphere in which young communicators find themselves is not friendly, and praise for good, rational deliberation is overlooked. If mentors praise young communicators, these newbies to the profession will relate "pleasure" with virtue.

For Aristotle, morality is obviously a continuing endeavor or activity. To choose the correct ethical action, communicators need to be habituated correctly—otherwise they will be unprepared to face ethical dilemmas in both their personal and professional lives. Unfortunately, young communicators may find themselves faced with colleagues and supervisors who are not striving for the good—only striving for money and ill-conceived happiness. Aristotle would ask the young communicator to choose a mean between foolhardiness and cowardliness; that mean is courage. Having the courage to learn, deliberate, and act ethically together go toward becoming "good," and with that good comes credibility for the communication professions. In other words, morality advances human "good."

■　■　■

Aristotle. 1998. *The Nicomachean Ethics.* Translated by David Ross, revised by J. L. Ackrill and J. O. Urmson. New York: Oxford University Press.

Barnes, J., ed. 1995. *The Cambridge Companion to Aristotle.* Cambridge, UK: Cambridge University Press.

McKeon, R., ed. 1947. *Introduction to Aristotle.* New York: Modern Library.

8

Friedrich Nietzsche
Becoming an Übermensch

CLIFFORD G. CHRISTIANS

Friedrich Nietzsche was one of the most influential European thinkers of the nineteenth century. His controversial ideas have been of interest to philosophers, sociologists, literary theorists, artists, and psychologists ever since. He was a philologist specializing in the Greek language and an amateur composer of music, so students of communication have a fascination with his work as well. He believed that since God was dead, morality no longer made sense. And he introduced other concepts still debated today such as *Übermensch* and the will to power.

He was born on October 15, 1844, near Leipzig, Germany, on the day of the Prussian king's (Friedrich Wilhelm IV) forty-ninth birthday, and was named after him. Nietzsche's father was a Lutheran minister, as were his grandfather and an uncle, and his paternal grandfather was a distinguished theologian. When Nietzsche was four, his father died from a brain disease; six months later his twenty-six-year-old brother died as well. His mother gave him special care even in his adult life, and his sister nursed him during his ill health in the last years before his death at the early age of fifty-six.

From the ages of fourteen to nineteen he attended a boarding school to prepare for a university education. He participated in a literature and music club during those years and became acquainted with Richard Wagner's music. He read the German romantic writings of Friedrich Hölderlin, and David Strauss's controversial *Life of Jesus Critically Examined.*

He entered the University of Bonn at nineteen and studied theology and also philology, especially the interpretation of classical and biblical texts. During the first semester he lost his faith and dropped theological studies. Inspired by the classics scholar Friedrich Wilhelm Ritschl, he transferred to the University of Leipzig after one year, and established a dazzling reputation as a student with published essays on Aristotle, Simonides, and others. At twenty-one he read the most momentous book of his life to that time, Arthur Schopenhauer's *The World as Will and Representation* (1818), an atheistic vision of the world in conjunction with his praise of music as an art form. When he met the composer Richard Wagner at twenty-three they shared an interest in Schopenhauer, and Nietzsche, who had composed music since he was a teenager, admired his musical genius. A language scholar married to Wagner's sister was a specialist in the Zoroastrian religion and its prophet Zarathustra (Zoroaster). These books and people influenced him deeply for the rest of his life.

Wilhelm Ritschl was so impressed with Nietzsche's brilliance that he recommended him at the astonishing age of twenty-four for a position as professor of classical philology at the University of Basel in Switzerland. Nietzsche was granted this appointment even before he had completed his doctorate or a certificate for teaching. However, his attempt to transfer that position to the philosophy department failed. At twenty-seven he brought his early influences together in his first book, *The Birth of Tragedy.* And over the next three years he published four studies of German culture, *The Unfashionable Observations*—including a response to the historian of religion, David Strauss. At age thirty-two he completed *Human, All-Too-Human.* But poor health—migraine headaches, violent vomiting, shortsightedness, and occasional blindness—necessitated his resignation in 1879 from the university after only ten years on the faculty.

For the decade following, he was officially stateless: he had renounced his Prussian citizenship upon moving to Switzerland, and never applied for Swiss citizenship. He lived with his mother, but traveled around various cities in Europe, staying in each only a few months at a time. During these nomadic years he wrote his main works, such as *Thus Spoke Zarathustra* (1883–1885), *Beyond Good and Evil* (1886), *On the Genealogy of Morals* (1887), *The Antichrist* (1888), *Ecce Homo* (1888), and *Nietzsche Contra Wagner* (1888).

In January 1889, Nietzsche suffered a mental breakdown that left him an invalid for the rest of his life. He may have had a syphilis infection, or a brain disease inherited from his father, or the drugs he used as a sedative may have been the cause. He was at first hospitalized and placed in a sanatorium, but his mother then took care of him in her home until she died, and his sister Elizabeth became the guardian of his manuscripts and archives since he was incapacitated. He died of a stroke on August 25, 1900.[1]

The "death of God" is Nietzsche's most famous phrase. It is repeated in several of his works. Developments in science and the increasing secularization of Europe had killed the Christian God who had served as the basis for morality and meaning in the West for a thousand years. Nietzsche does not argue that science has proved God's existence to be false and therefore atheism is true. In fact, he is concerned that without a theistic perspective, there is no coherent ground for truth or a universal framework. Life is tragic because we are all alone in the universe without a higher being to help us in our suffering.

Nietzsche welcomed secularism and believed the world had become as non-Christian as it was before Christ. But he was dissatisfied with the easygoing, irresponsible secularism of his contemporaries. He revolted against the shallow secularism of his day that was weak and facile compared to the artistic style of Greek civilization. Nietzsche considered humanity's gravest problem to be finding a profound philosophy of life to replace the antiquated Christian one.

On the Genealogy of Morals (1887) contends that Christian morality was formed from revenge, resentment, hatred, and cowardice. It is a sickness that lives by condemning others as wicked. In addition, Nietzsche argues, Christian morality stifles our natural inclinations as evil and is therefore unhealthy. And the priesthood is scandalous— weak people gaining power for themselves by controlling even weaker people. Western culture has suffered for two thousand years under a moral system born of sickness. Over against the traditional belief that ethics was essential for moral order, Nietzsche contended that moral values had become worthless.

Therefore, he threw himself fully into artistic experience for replacing religious experience. Art was sacred for him, inspiring us and preserving for us the best in human values. Art gave nonreligious existence the qualities of eternity. Art provides release from the tensions of everyday life. It consoles and refreshes. In the Preface to *The Birth of Tragedy*, Nietzsche writes: "Art represents the highest task and the

---

1. For the biographical details summarized in the section above, see Robert Wicks, "Friedrich Nietzsche."

truly metaphysical activity of this life" (31–32). "Nietzsche insisted that art, particularly music, should be approached with the same earnestness with which St. Paul, Augustine, and Luther had approached religion."[2]

Übermensch is a central idea in Nietzsche also. Typically translated as *superman* or *superhuman,* this is his ideal version of human beings in contrast to the degraded centerpiece of liberal and socialist politics. It is a higher mode of being, a more-than-man. No living person has reached the Superman level; this possibility is for the future. Superman does not control and terrorize. He is not brutal, but uses his power to give meaning and beauty to life. Nietzsche did not seek to destroy culture, but to attain a higher type of culture. And for an elevated culture, humans themselves must be elevated. Since he did not find that higher type of human being, Nietzsche created him.

But Nietzsche's fondness for Napoleon promoted a warrior understanding of Superman. By the First World War, he was interpreted as supporting right-wing German militarism, and 150,000 copies of *Thus Spoke Zarathustra* were printed for the Kaiser's army. Later, during the 1930s, aspects of Nietzsche's thought were espoused by the Nazis and Italian Fascists. It was possible for Nazi interpreters to assemble, quite selectively, various passages from Nietzsche's writings whose juxtaposition appeared to justify war, aggression, and domination for the sake of nationalistic and racial self-glorification.

In his commitment to everyday life above scholastic philosophy, Nietzsche's work is explicitly psychological. Carl Jung and Sigmund Freud both were influenced by him. As Nietzsche would put it, the principle of life is a higher concern than rational knowledge. Morality for him was naturalistic, rooted in the vital impulses of our ordinary existence. Until his break in his later years with Richard Wagner, he admired Wagner's music for expressing loneliness and suffering so profoundly. As noted in the subtitle of *The Birth of Tragedy* (*Out of the Spirit of Music*), published in 1872, he advocated release of artistic energies in order to bring joy into our painful and decadent existence.

His most important analysis of human psychology is in his concept of the will to power, which for Nietzsche (1880) is the motivation underlying all human behavior. His argument is rooted in the

---

2. Heinz Bluhm, "The Young Nietzsche and the Secular City," 726.

Greek history he knew well. Greek heroes were not content with simply living; they wanted power and greatness. They died young and risked their lives in warfare and competitive games. On the other hand, badness is lived by slave morality; Greek slaves, Jewish slaves in Egypt, Christians persecuted by Rome were weak, sick and pathetic. The higher person lives above the herd and is a creator of values. The Jeremy Bentham–John Stuart Mill tradition that claimed people wanted happiness first of all was popular in his day; but Nietzsche saw the "will to power" as a deeper and more general view of human behavior. The Platonic and monotheistic traditions that claimed people wanted a unified good, he relegated to the minority.

Thus Spoke Zarathustra (1883–1885), a philosophical work of fiction, is one of Nietzsche's most famous books and explicitly includes "will to power" for the first time. While antagonistic to Judeo-Christian monotheism, it is a manifesto to strong-willed, proud, self-confident human beings who are psychologically healthy and live beyond the ordinary. Zarathustra is the exemplar of the higher person, come down from the mountain to speak to people in the marketplace. We ought to follow this thought experiment, Nietzsche says: imagine life does not end at death but will repeat itself in exactly the same way for all eternity as you are living it now. In *Beyond Good and Evil,* published the following year (1886), he challenges those who condemn exploitation, destruction, and injury to the weak. When humans pour out their full energy, Nietzsche argues, there is danger and pain. What counts as acceptable behavior depends on whether someone is sickly and weak, or healthy and overflowing with life.

Nietzsche's specific challenge for communications is to keep aesthetics and ethics together. In questioning God's existence and with it the viability of moral commands, he turned to aesthetic values that need no supernatural sanction. We can speak of beauty, he says, without implying that anything ought to be beautiful or that anybody must create the beautiful. In *The Birth of Tragedy*, Nietzsche puts it this way: "Only as an aesthetic phenomenon are life and the world justified eternally" (5, 24). In summarizing the postmodern argument against ethics, Zygmunt Bauman uses Nietzsche's perspective: ethics has been replaced by aesthetics.[3] In other words, what

---

3. Zygmunt Bauman, *Postmodern Ethics*, 178–79.

Nietzsche thought in the nineteenth century should be the case, as a matter of fact has happened and is true of the twenty-first century in the West.

At this time in history, morality has appeared to reach the end of the line. The social fashion is to be emancipated from moral standards and to disavow moral responsibility. Popular culture gets caught up in the technological imperative, producing the visually interesting, creating programs of artistic wholeness, but driven by the conditions of aesthetics rather than ethics. In defining today's society as aesthetic space, popular arts of the eye and ear re-create a spectacle in which amusement values override all other considerations. Cultural relativity is unquestioned and celebrated—that is, the right and valid are only known in local space and native languages. A context that is intelligible, an argument that is valid, a television entertainment program that is artistically genuine, and judgments of right and wrong, are accepted as such by a culture's internal criteria. And therefore these concepts, propositions, and judgments are considered to have no validity elsewhere.

Perspectives on public communication that integrate ethics and aesthetics are the best antidote. Aesthetics is an important feature of the communication age, but the arts can demonstrate a broader understanding of the human condition. Rather than surrender ethics to aesthetics, Johan Huizinga's *Homo Ludens* and Josef Pieper's *Leisure: The Basis of Culture* make them co-constitutive of one another.

■ ■ ■

Bauman, Zygmunt. 1993. *Postmodern Ethics.* Oxford, UK: Blackwell.

Bluhm, Heinz. 1969. "The Young Nietzsche and the Secular City." *MLN* (German issue) 84, no. 5: 716–33.

Kaufmann, Walter. 1968. *Nietzsche: Philosopher, Psychologist, Antichrist.* New York: Vintage.

Leiter, Brian. 2002. *Routledge Guidebook to Nietzsche on Morality.* London: Routledge.

Nietzsche, Friedrich. 1966. *Beyond Good and Evil.* Translated by W. Kaufmann. New York: Random House. Original work published in 1886.

———. 1967. *The Birth of Tragedy.* Translated by W. Kaufmann. New York: Vintage. Original work published in 1872.

————. 1967. *On the Genealogy of Morals.* Translated by W. Kaufmann and R. J. Hollingdale. New York: Random House. Original work published in 1887.

————. 2006. *Thus Spoke Zarathustra: A Book for All and None.* Translated by Adrian Del Caro. Cambridge, UK: Cambridge University Press. Original work published in 1883–1885.

————. 1967. *The Will to Power: Attempt at a Revaluation of all Values.* Translated by W. Kaufmann. New York: Random House. Originally published in 1901; expanded edition, 1906. [Published posthumously by his sister Elizabeth Forster-Nietzsche.]

Wicks, Robert. 2004. "Friedrich Nietzsche." In Edward N. Zalta, ed., *The Stanford Encyclopedia of Philosophy.* http://plato.stanford.edu/archives/fall2007/entries/wicks/.

9

Machiavelli
Pragmatic Realism

JOHN C. MERRILL

What, you might ask, is Machiavelli (1469–1527) doing in a book such as this? What did he, or can he, teach us about ethics? And, what's more—what is he doing in this part of the book representing the Egoistic Stance? All good questions. Let us look briefly at each one in order.

Why Machiavelli in an ethics book? Because, in spite of his renown in the area of pragmatics rather than ethics, he did in fact deal with ethics—the ethics of self-enhancement, of the importance of ends, and the difference between private and public ethics. We'll go into that later. But it is almost impossible to deal with ethics without having to consider alternative options for action that will help us achieve our ends.

Machiavelli can teach us much about ethics, about the difficulties of making ethical decisions and about the importance of consequences. In fact, many writers include him as a utilitarian because of his practical approach to ethics. He is perhaps the most important writer on the consideration of "ends" and the necessity of pragmatic "means." Success is the key word in Machiavellian ethics.

What is Machiavelli doing here as an example of the Egoistic Stance? It seems natural that "Old Nick" (as he was called by Catholics of his age) should represent the stance of personal and institutional success. Egoism generated his public ethics, the ethics of self-fulfillment, and a strong survival motivation. The ends justify the means, as the saying goes. But what are the proper ends? Those, says Machiavelli, that please the ego and satisfy the basic desires of the ethical agent.

The world of communication today is filled with the presence of Machiavelli: gaining power and keeping it; setting goals and reaching them; persuading people by any and all means; respecting normal ethics when they work, disregarding them when they don't; being goal oriented and self-confident; being certain of one's own actions; sharing power reluctantly; believing that might is right; and camouflaging weakness by assertive communication.

Machiavelli represents the extreme opposite of those thinkers in this book who are called communitarians. And his stance is certainly not one of altruism. He is even more fundamental than other egoists and self-development thinkers profiled in this section of the book. Machiavelli's best-known book, *The Prince* (1514), set the political stage for the pragmatic, expedient, and success-oriented practitioner in social relations—and that includes the communicator who provides grist for the mill of social thinking and action.

In the broad field of mass communication today, Machiavellian thinking is prominent, and is often the main, viable ethical stance. For example, journalism's power is used variously in different societies, but the common factor everywhere is contained in this basic question: How can we achieve our ends? In the United States, a businesslike, impersonal, bottom-line-oriented corporate journalism has grown greatly since the nineteenth century. Increasingly it has become a journalism of groups, chains, and ever-growing media networks where decisions are made in boardrooms by lawyers and businessmen and businesswomen instead of in newsrooms by editors. The goal is viability and profits. If journalistic quality has to be sacrificed for these ends, then so be it. Even a poor newspaper is better than none. Raw Machiavellianism at work.

This mentality is not new. American journalism has always been practical, competitive, success-driven, and power-hungry. It has only become more expansive, more efficient in its business operations, and more concerned with "democratizing" than in the past. It could be said that Thomas Hobbes's *Leviathan* has today become the Press.

American communicators, from politicians to bloggers to TV newspersons, show Machiavellian tendencies. Although normally we associate these tendencies with evil or unethical ends, this may be somewhat unfair. Even the most socially conscious, altruistic editor may use Machiavellian tactics from time to time. We must remember that *ends can be good.* For instance, if a communicator is attempting to get people to stop smoking, he or she may use means that are propagandistic, biased, or misleading to a degree—all to bring about *an ethical end.*

Niccolò Machiavelli was an Italian political philosopher, poet, playwright, and historian born in Florence in 1469. He developed the idea that political leaders are not bound by conventional morality and insisted that the cunning use of power is of the utmost importance. He divided his life between an active political period when he was a consultant for princes and a time of retirement when he did most of his writing. He was a good communicator, a good reporter, and a good historian. He was also a keen observer, a careful listener, and a skilled debater. His preserved reports from France and Germany during the first decade of the sixteenth century evidence a good understanding of institutions and politics.

Unlike the famous legalist German philosopher, Immanuel Kant, Machiavelli cared deeply about consequences—and not those bringing the greatest happiness or good, such as those the utilitarians embraced—just those that bring success. Don't worry about what most people might see as the right thing to do. Do what is necessary to achieve your ends in a particular case. Tell the truth when it will benefit you and your objective; forget the truth—or bend it—when you think it is necessary. Pragmatism, not moralism, was at the base of Machiavelli's ethics.

But Machiavelli was not the simple exemplar of evil, the so-called Anti-Christ that many called him. He may have preached pragmatics instead of ethics, but he knew better. And in many aspects of his personal life, he was better. He acknowledged normal, humanistic ethics assumed by the Church and others of his day. In fact he was the first to really differentiate "private" ethics from "public" ethics. In his consulting of political leaders he emphasized "public" ethics, the kind of pragmatic ethics that would lead to success.

In his own life, he practiced normal or "private" ethics—a more humane, caring, principled version of ethics. An example of "public" ethics: willingness to kill while serving in an army, whereas killing would not be ethical in one's private life. Often, said Machiavelli, in order for an institution to survive and thrive, one must resort to public or expedience ethics. He would obviously apply this "public" ethics to one's desire for success as an institutional communicator.

But what about an individual, noninstitutional communicator? One cannot be sure, of course, but he would probably say that if one's objective was commendable or noble, then it would be ethical for one to achieve it by any means. Resort to normal practices and standard ethics first, he would say, but if those won't work, then use any means that will work in order to achieve success.

Machiavelli would want the communicator, especially the public or mass communicator, to be a virtuoso, a person who relies on what he called *virtù*—ingenuity, decisiveness, and cleverness. A journalist, for instance, should be persistent, determined, risk-taking, and innovative. In *The Prince*, Machiavelli said that public leaders should be as strong as lions and as cunning as foxes. However, he said, virtuosity, revealing our freedom and stemming from our cunning, is naturally impaired. Machiavelli believed that freedom is restricted by Fortune (*fortuna*), or chance, which determines so much of what happens; so for the communicator it is useless to expect to act freely any more than half the time.

An aspect of communication freedom considered important to Machiavelli is the freedom to choose tactics for success. As for responsibility, a public communicator's responsibility is to succeed—to achieve the desired objective. Regarding public service communication, Machiavelli would say this should be a guiding principle: Help others if it helps you. Be kind and caring of others if doing so improves your image or helps you reach your objective. Do not waste time on others if nothing positive for you is likely to result. Machiavelli's realist perspective took into account the way society functioned in reality and how people behaved in that reality; he was not concerned with providing a blueprint for honorable behavior or how society *should* function.

Machiavelli would pay little attention to what we normally think of as communication ethics, for he was a firm believer in pragmatics. If he would fit into normal ethical theories, he would probably be a consequentialist, a teleologist, or a utilitarian. But Machiavellian ethicists would not be utilitarians like Jeremy Bentham or John Stuart Mill, concerned with maximizing the happiness of others; instead, they would want to increase their own happiness or the happiness of those in their institution.

There is much about Machiavelli that reminds one of Nietzsche, in that he recognized the value of self-development and power, and a strong will to power. Except, of course, Nietzsche was a humanist injected with intuitive or mystical insights, a far cry from Machiavelli's realistic pragmatism. But Machiavelli did stress the person. Look inside, develop the self so as to transcend one's essence—important for

Machiavelli, more important for Nietzsche. Certainly, like Nietzsche and Plato before him, Machiavelli had no illusions of social equality. He definitely saw a structured society with activists and pacifists, with leaders and followers, with rich and poor, and with the powerful and the powerless. And for him, as for Nietzsche, the individual person comes before the group; as the individual persons evolve, so evolves the society. No communitarianism here.

Communitarians today often see consequentialists—or utilitarians —as little more than egocentric individuals caring little for bene– volence and altruism. This may be true of some consequentialists (and Machiavelli is an example), but most philosophers would see utilitarian thinkers such as J. S. Mill as altruists, as caring for the happiness of others.

On the other hand, Machiavelli is an example of an egoistic utilitarian, mainly interested in bringing success and happiness to the actor. Such pragmatic consequentialism from Kant's cold and a priori legalist perspective would be a surrender of principle, an abdication of ethical responsibility and nothing more than personal aggrandizement and rationalization.

Kant is further from Machiavelli than perhaps any other philosopher. John Stuart Mill is little closer. For one thing, Mill cherished freedom and individualism and a relativistic ethics which would allow for a certain amount of Machiavellianism. But whereas Mill would say, "seek the good in your own way," Machiavelli would say, "seek success in your own way."

Altruistic ethics, for Machiavelli, would be counterproductive to the public communicator such as a journalist. Such ethical concern would lead to a schizophrenic state of mind that would result in overcaution, cowardice, inaction, and compromise. It would replace firm decision with indecision. And it would result often in not telling stories that should be told and in biasing stories for "the sake of fairness." Not that Machiavelli would be against biasing stories; it would be fine *if it leads to the communicator's success.*

Machiavelli would have supported public relations activities in the modern world—provided that the public relations practitioners were dedicated, authentic, success-oriented propagandists. He also would have observed that the primary objective of the public communicator is manipulation of minds, especially in the public relations industry. Machiavelli would also have noted that the state and the media cooperate in keeping people fearful and uncertain of the future.

He believed that people are generally ungrateful, eager to avoid trouble, and are exceedingly selfish, but *passively* selfish. As such, they need directive communication, uplifting messages, and superficial entertainment. In order to keep the people content and passive, give them images, appearances, and a little hope now and then.

Believing that people care little for substance, for reality, or for power, Machiavelli would have communicators create the world for them, set their daily agenda of concern, and pacify them with the drug of entertainment. This is the raw power of communication, held in the hands of the public communicators and the institutionalized mass media. Many of the people want to appear knowledgeable and sophisticated, and this principle, of course, would explain the great success of "image-builders," such as political consultants and public relations practitioners.

Machiavelli was a pragmatic realist. His ethics or "nonethics" is certainly not of the mainstream—especially the religious mainstream. But it is here with us; its success orientation permeates entire societies and cannot be ignored. Communicators seeking success, limited or widespread, will find its magnetic pull powerful. If nothing else, Machiavelli draws attention to the dark side of ethics and exposes us to our egoistic rationalizations.

Machiavellian communication ethics differs significantly from communication informed by Christian principles, based on caring and compassionate dialogue. The Christian communicator would be an altruist and would also focus on the transcendent "beyond," deemphasizing worldly power (being *in* the world but not *of* it) and thereby unconcerned for Machiavellian virtuosity.

Communicating in the directive, polemical style of Machiavelli is, fortunately, not for everybody, but it is possibly more common than is generally supposed. A more altruistic and humanistic communication ethics undoubtedly prevails in the American rhetorical arena, but beneath the surface there is a sizable egoistic and pragmatic force of Machiavellianism that gives rise to serious ethical questions.

■　■　■

Machiavelli, Niccolò. *The Discourses.* Many editions.

———. *The Prince.* Many editions.

Kahn, Victoria. 1994. *Machiavellian Rhetoric.* Princeton, N.J.: Princeton University Press.

Merrill, John C. 1998. *The Princely Press: Machiavelli on American Journalism.* Lanham, Md.: University Press of America.

10

Camus
The Rebellious Spirit

DAVID J. GUNKEL

> For if there is a sin against life, it consists perhaps not so much in despairing of life as in hoping for another life and in eluding the implacable grandeur of this life.
>
> —Albert Camus, "Summer in Algiers"
> (*The Myth of Sisyphus and Other Essays*, 153)

Albert Camus was born on November 7, 1913, in Mondovi, a small village near the seaport city of Bonê (present-day Annaba) in French Algeria. His father, who was recalled to military service during the initial stages of the First World War, died less than a year later at the battle of Marne. Camus's mother raised both him and his brother, after relocating the family to Algiers. As the child of a working-class French family in a North African city, Camus witnessed firsthand the conflicts of race, ethnicity, class, and religion that would come to define so much of the twentieth century. And it was in this multicultural environment that Camus spent his formative years, eventually graduating from the University of Algiers in 1936.

Camus's literary career began almost immediately after graduation. His first book, a collection of essays, called *L'envers et l'endroit* (*Betwixt and Between or The Wrong Side and the Right Side*) was published in 1937, establishing the young writer's reputation in his hometown. During this time, Camus also founded a theater troupe and worked as a journalist for a French-language daily, the *Alger Républicain.* Shortly after the outbreak of the Second World War, Camus relocated to France. He became involved with the Resistance, wrote for the newspaper *Combat,* and published, in 1942, two books that would eventually come to establish his international reputation, *L'étranger* (*The Stranger*) and *Le mythe de Sisyphe* (*The Myth of Sisyphus*).

After the liberation of France, Camus continued his work as an editor at *Combat,* published several plays, and became one of the luminaries of Parisian intellectual life alongside Jean-Paul Sartre and Simone de Beauvoir. By the late 1940s, Camus had retired from his position at the paper and dedicated himself to his literary career, publishing *Le peste* (*The Plague*), an allegorical novel of the Nazi occupation, and *L'homme révolté* (*The Rebel*). The latter, which appeared in 1951, comprised a book-length analysis of the nature of rebellion and revolutionary violence and instituted something of an unanticipated upheaval in Camus's own life. The book not only precipitated a split with Sartre and his company but lead to Camus's exclusion from the community of contemporary European intellectuals, many of whom judged the work to be reactionary. Camus attempted, in part, to respond to this fallout in *Le chute* (*The Fall*), which was published in 1956.

Despite or perhaps because of these controversies, Camus was awarded the Nobel Prize for literature in 1957. In honoring this relatively young writer (at age forty-four Camus was one of the youngest individuals to be awarded the prize for literature), the Nobel committee cited Camus's persistent efforts to illuminate the problems of the human conscience. Although Camus considered himself to be at midcareer at the time of the award, he died just three years later, on January 4, 1960, in an automobile accident.

Strictly speaking, Camus had always considered himself more of a writer concerned with exploring philosophical themes, than a philosopher. Consequently, finding the articulation of an ethics in his writings requires some interpretation. In fact, one could say that Camus is less of an innovator in twentieth-century moral thought than he is its expositor and dramatist. Saying this does not diminish his unique contribution. On the contrary, it is simply an honest statement about the significance of his work, which is a moral posture that Camus himself both advocated and exemplified. In his various publications, whether they have the form of fiction, drama, or essay, Camus takes the innovations of modern European philosophers like René Descartes, Immanuel Kant, and Friedrich Nietzsche (all of whom, in one way or another, sought to define the proper limits of human knowledge) and pursues them, oftentimes against these thinkers' own intentions and conclusions, to their logical, if not extreme, ends. If, as Camus explains in *The Myth of Sisyphus,* we remain within the strictly defined limits of what can be properly known, one can only conclude that there is no transcendental authority that can bestow any higher significance to life as it is lived and experienced. Or to put it in that famous Nietzschean shorthand, it appears that God is dead. Camus wanted to know what follows from affirming this fact honestly, that is, without recourse to any external assurances or fantastic metaphysical appeals, whether religious, philosophical, psychological, or otherwise. Does it, for example, mean that all morality is suspended and, as Fyodor Dostoevsky's character Ivan Karamazov concludes, everything is permitted?

For Camus, the place where this rather heady question comes to be experienced is in the face of death—the death of the self and the death of the other. This is articulated explicitly in the first lines of the preface that Camus contributed to the 1955 English translation of *The Myth of Sisyphus.* "For me *The Myth of Sisyphus* marks the beginning of an idea which I was to pursue in *The Rebel.* It attempts to resolve the problem of suicide, as *The Rebel* attempts to resolve that of murder, in both cases without the aid of eternal values which, temporarily perhaps, are absent or distorted in contemporary Europe" (v). And for Camus, it is suicide that takes precedence both conceptually and literally. *The Myth of Sisyphus,* which precedes *The Rebel* by some nine years, begins with the following rather provocative statement: "There is but one truly serious philosophical problem, and that is suicide" (1955, 3). For Camus, therefore, suicide is the philosophical problem par excellence. If there is no god, or, what amounts to the same, if I am at all uncertain whether there is anything above and beyond this terrestrial existence, then life can have no deeper meaning outside of what confronts me here and now. And if this is the case, one might justifiably ask, why bother living? Why not simply end it all? For Camus, this position is ultimately untenable and unjustified. One can, he argues, only make this decision, if he or she already posits value in and appeals to some transcendental fantasy. But if there is no such thing (or, what is effectively the same, if it is impossible to know with any certitude whether there is such a thing), then one has no justification for judging this life deficient. If we are brutally honest with ourselves, we have to conclude that this life, understood within its necessary and finite limitations, is worth it, because that is all there is and all there will ever be.

Camus illustrates this point by way of the parable to which his essay's title makes reference. Sisyphus, a well-known character from Greek mythology, was condemned by the gods to roll a boulder up the side of a mountain, only to have it tumble down again and again ad infinitum. As long as Sisyphus appeals to some external justification for this torture or posits value in some transcendental explanation, we can only imagine that he is unhappy and frustrated. However, if Sisyphus remains honest about his own situation and strictly attends to what confronts him, then all there is to his existence is this toil itself. Following from this insight, the seemingly infinite labor is no longer some unjustifiable torture; it constitutes the very fabric of his life. Consequently, "one must," as Camus writes in the final line of the essay, "imagine Sisyphus happy" (1955, 123).

Although providing an adequate response to the question of suicide, Camus's solution runs into considerable difficulties when one considers his or her relationship to and responsibility for others. To put it in rather blunt terms, why not take the life of another, especially if all I can be sure of is my own continued existence and experiences? In other words, what if anything is to prevent an individual from imposing his or her will on everyone else? Why not, like Mersault, the disaffected protagonist of Camus's *The Stranger*, kill the other? This problem is not, it is important to note, unique to Camus. It affects all those ethical theories that are ultimately based on and derived from a fundamental privilege of the individual (e.g., deontologism, utilitarianism, consequentialism, virtue ethics, etc.). And Camus takes up and directly addresses this problem in *The Rebel*.

"Is it possible," Camus asks at the beginning of this book-length essay, "to find a rule of conduct outside the realm of religion and its absolute values? That is the question raised by rebellion" (1953, 21). For Camus, rebellion is a moral issue. Already in *The Myth of Sisyphus*, rebellion is conceptualized as the proper response of the human individual in the face of the absurd disjunction between one's human reality and the forever distant world outside it. But the individual's rebellion against such absurdity immediately encounters its own limit, that is, the same rebellious spirit exercised by others.

In other words, our individual response to the perceived injustice in the universe is immediately limited by our responsibility to others, who have the right to a similar response. Because of this, Camus concludes, human solidarity is founded on rebellion and rebellion can only be justified by this solidarity. Any rebellious undertaking that is not grounded in and responsible to the larger human community, even to one's perceived enemies, devolves into violence and murder, or what Camus terms "revolution." "In our daily trials," Camus writes, "rebellion plays the same role as does the 'cogito' in the realm of thought: it is the first piece of evidence. But this evidence lures the individual from his solitude. It founds its first value on the whole human race. I rebel—therefore we exist" (1953, 22).

It is with this "we exist" that Camus's thinking necessarily engages with communication and communication ethics. And in this regard, Camus comes very close to the work of American communication theorist James Carey. In his seminal essay, "A Cultural Approach to Communication," Carey characterizes two nonexclusive viewpoints by which to investigate the activity of communication—transmission and ritual. The "transmission view of communication," Carey argues, consists of the standard sender/receiver model that is so prevalent in the discipline and initially formalized in Claude Shannon and Warren Weaver's mathematical theory. The "ritual view of communication," by contrast, introduces an alternative understanding, one where communication is defined in recognition of its etymological connection to "community," "communion," and "commonality"— a connection that is literally grounded in the very concept of the common. According to Carey, the ritual view of communication is interested in defining how distinct human communities come to be organized around commonly shared values and beliefs, and how this takes place in and by various forms of communicative interaction (1992, 18–19). In a similar vein, Camus's The Rebel is concerned with the manner by which distinct human communities (or what he calls "human solidarity") coalesce around common understanding and values. Because these common features cannot be grounded in some transcendental and external authority, they must be negotiated and renegotiated in and by various forms of communicative interactions. In other words, communication is the only means by which shared experiences can be articulated and human communities can be organized. Consequently, for Camus, communication, community, and common moral understanding are indissolubly connected and necessarily interdependent.

In retrospect, it is possible to overlay this insight on Camus's own life. Having grown up in French Algiers, the young Camus was constantly in the position of having to negotiate and renegotiate the different communities to which he belonged. On the one hand, he supported and often wrote (as a journalist) in defense of the exercise of French colonial power in North Africa. On the other hand, he clearly empathized with and actively sought to advance the civil rights of the predominantly Muslim community upon whom this power was imposed. Similarly, *The Rebel*, in which Camus sought to differentiate legitimate claims to rebellion from the kinds of revolutionary violence that had been perpetrated throughout the mid–twentieth century, had the effect of alienating him from the company of his European contemporaries, many of whom interpreted the text as an indictment of their common social and political values. And this is perhaps Camus's final moral instruction, one that addresses the very (im)possibility of finality in ethical matters. If rebellion is, as Camus concludes at the end of *The Rebel*, a never-ending and dynamic process, then it must be an ongoing struggle that can never be exhausted and that must continually learn to question its own outcomes and conclusions. Such persistent rebellion constitutes what Jacques Derrida, another Algerian-born French thinker, calls an "interminable analysis" (1981, 42). Although this might sound like some kind of moral relativism, Camus demonstrates, in both his writings and his own life, how such "relativism" is itself responsible for, and the necessary condition of, any ethic that is honest about its own situation and limits.

■　■　■

Camus, Albert. 1937. *L'envers et l'endroit (Betwixt and Between or The Wrong Side and the Right Side)*. Alger: Charlot.

———. 1947. *Caligula and Cross Purpose*. Translated by Stuart Gilbert. New York: New Directions. Original work published in 1944 (Paris: Gallimard).

———. 1948. *The Plague*. Translated by Stuart Gilbert. New York: Knopf. Original work published in 1947 (Paris: Gallimard).

———. 1953. *The Rebel: An Essay on Man in Revolt*. Translated by Anthony Bower. London: Hamilton. Original work published in 1951 (Paris: Gallimard).

————. 1955. *The Myth of Sisyphus and Other Essays.* Translated by Justin O'Brien. London: Hamilton. Original work published in 1942 (Paris: Gallimard).

————. 1957. *The Fall.* Translated by Justin O'Brien. New York: Knopf. Original work published in 1956 (Paris: Gallimard).

————. 1988. *The Stranger.* Translated by Matthew Ward. New York: Knopf. Original work published in 1942 (Paris: Gallimard).

Carey, James. 1981. *Communication as Culture.* New York: Routledge.

Derrida, Jacques. 1972. *Positions.* Translated by Alan Bass. Chicago: University of Chicago Press. Original work published in 1972 (Paris: Les Editions de Minuit).

Kautilya of India
Social Egoism

JOHN C. MERRILL

Some have called Kautilya (also known as Chanakya and Visnu-gupta), an Indian thinker of the fourth century BCE, the "Machiavelli of India." Kautilya taught at Taxila University, was a noted economist and philosopher, and served as an adviser to princes and kings. He is thought to be responsible for the unification of India. He at least played a significant role in establishing the empire.

Kautilya gained significance as prime minister under the first Maurya emperor, Chandragupta (c. 390–340 BCE). Little is known of him, but we do know that he was a pragmatist who shared many similarities with the much later Machiavelli of Florence. He recognized that leaders must get power and keep it, using any means necessary. His best-known work was *Arthashastra* ("Science of Polity") written in Sanskrit. It was a work of political realism and dealt with his governmental theories and advice to those rulers he believed to have complete control. He might be called the first authoritarian political philosopher. For him, the ruler (steeped in wisdom and social concern) should do whatever was necessary to succeed in his program.

Kautilya's political philosophy contributed greatly to the Maurya emperor's desire to unify India. In fact, many often refer to Kautilya as the "father of the nation." In spite of his authoritarian leanings, he believed that leaders should be available to the people, stay busy, set a good example, listen to advisers, reward loyalty and good work, and have little tolerance for lazy and inefficient workers. He had little sympathy for excuses, and found many and varied ways to punish disobedience and sloppiness. He was a strict disciplinarian, an impatient critic, a champion of success, and a firm defender of his own interests.

In spite of his harsh philosophy, he had a deep respect for the common people, and—like Plato at about the same time—wanted a governmental system, hierarchical in nature, that would provide a stable and satisfying life for the masses. Kautilya could be termed a "hard-nosed" realist. He knew what he wanted to accomplish and forged ahead to achieve his goal. But he was not impulsive, not one to act without thinking through the problem facing him. He wanted a unified and cooperative India, one that would put a stop to all the tribal infighting that continuously fractured the subcontinent.

It seemed to him that the various regional chieftains were harming their own people through their noncooperative attitudes and often bloody confrontations with their neighbors. Kautilya was determined to stop this internecine fighting and place all of India under a powerful and stabilizing ruler.

The unification of the country was not an easy task. It would take somebody who could appeal to the local rulers, using cunning and even deception, to forge an agreement to such an ambitious scheme. Kautilya was just such a person with the necessary recipe. He was egoistic. He was pragmatic. He was determined and forceful. He was tireless as a debater, skillful as a persuader, and unusually effective in his appeal for centralization of power.

In comparison with Machiavelli, Kautilya had a more socially oriented philosophy, perhaps a more humanistic one, that had the good of the common people at its core. He was not simply a military advocate, but had as his end the betterment of society in general. He thought persuasion was equally as effective as warfare, probably more so. But to achieve his objectives he would use any means that would work.

Kautilya used many methods of deception, including lying, exaggeration, and censorship. His end—the unification of India—was far more important to him than the means that he used. This strategic goal benefited the people and led to whatever tactics would work to bring about some kind of national mentality. He went about this task with fervor and persistence, although he faced many opponents. If there was anyone who believed in himself and his capacity for achieving his goals, it was surely Kautilya.

In fact, many might consider him more of a utilitarian (in the modern sense) than an egoist. There is no doubt but that he considered the happiness of society—in this case all of India—as his ethical objective. But he felt that without his own determination, skill, and cunning, this broad social utilitarian objective could not be achieved. He might be called a social egoist.

Kautilya's ethics could not be called normative. There were really no rules for the leaders. For the people, of course, there was one rule: obey the leader. Results, not rules, were the key. In spite of his concern for social stability and happiness, he had doubts about the trustworthiness of the people. He believed that they should be watched closely, and his Brahmin spy system was elaborate and successful. He advised the leader to have spies everywhere, informing him of plots, rumors, and plans for conspiracies. His advice: trust nobody, watch everybody, punish enemies, and reward allies. He had high expectations of the king setting a good example for his subjects. The king should be energetic and resourceful. Laziness, for Kautilya, was a danger to the state and to the leader and would open one to the dictates of enemies. The king, with general public happiness in mind, would also structure the life of his subjects, even setting certain activities for each segment of the day. In the *Arthashastra,* writing of the qualities required for a leader, Kautilya says that the happiness and welfare of his subjects lie with the king's happiness.

The good king has the highest qualities of intellect and leadership. A leader has a certain charisma that attracts followers. He is of a noble family and is intelligent, righteous, truthful, disciplined, honest, and shrewd. He shows gratitude to those who help him, has lofty objectives, is stronger than neighboring rulers, and has intelligent and competent ministers. In peaceful activities he is effective, but when at war he is skillful and determined. He is dignified at all times, avoiding greed, anger, fickleness, and gossip. He would listen to the elders, taking their counsel in most cases.

Kautilya advised against addiction to strong drink, lusting after women, gambling, and hunting. He also warned against laziness and social uselessness. Self-discipline was extremely important to Kautilya, and intelligent motivation was the key virtue for a leader's subjects.

Kautilya viewed good communication as essential. Communication was power and should be used with skill by those who held leadership positions. The average person, he believed, could be swayed to accept almost anything if he or she received a correctly framed message that appealed to his or her selfish interests. He urged the leader (the "rajarshi" or "maharaj"— wise and virtuous king) to try to persuade first, and to use more forceful methods only if the first attempt failed. A good debater and skilled rhetorician himself, he believed that language was the primary tool for good and viable government. However, he was realistic enough to know that it could not always work. War, for Kautilya, was sometimes necessary, but he believed that good persuasion (propaganda) was always preferable to the destruction that resulted from fighting.

Kautilya was probably the first in Indian history to be an unashamed promoter of realpolitik. He was a realist and a pragmatist and had little use for customary forms of traditional tactics—unless they would achieve his ends. His use of the language was exceptional, a very formal style consisting of clear arguments. He advocated propaganda of all kinds, from the darkest to the lighter shades, and viewed language as a potent instrument for getting what you want— on par with military action.

His ethical philosophy might be summed up like this: One should have an objective in mind that promotes social progress and happiness and should be prepared to use any methods necessary to reach this objective. In short: whatever works is ethical. Certainly this ethics is a far cry from that of Immanuel Kant, whose legalistic philosophy would oppose the use of unethical means to achieve even an ethical end. Lying and deception was quite acceptable for Kautilya, anathema for Kant. Today, many would consider Kautilya more of a pragmatist than ethicist, although others who accept John Stuart Mill's greatest happiness principle might excuse his dubious means and praise him for his efforts to bring about general social happiness.

Many of Kautilya's ideas seem overly cruel and harsh to the modern ethicist. He could be excessive in his advice to the Indian rulers. For example, he advocated telling lies, using deception and cunning, spreading rumors, hiding your identity when needed, playing one person or group against another, and using threats to avoid a fight, but fighting if the situation demanded it. He advised his kings to fight to win when they had to fight, and to take advantage of enemies when they are having trouble with their own people. The time to strike, said Kautilya, is when your opponent is weak.

Few ethicists would condone Kautilya's tactics for getting rid of an enemy who is scheming against you. For example, he advised the king to take a variety of actions, including poisoning someone's rice and water, stabbing someone in the back, rigging walls to fall on someone, making someone fall into a pit containing pointed spears, injuring or killing someone in their sleep, and disguising himself as a woman to kill another person.

It could be, however, that even in today's world many serious ethicists might justify such extreme actions if they believed the enemy was a serious threat to society or the global civilization. For example, various attempts were made to kill Adolf Hitler by Germans who thought him a menace (e.g., Dietrich Bonhoeffer and Erwin Rommel), taking precisely the Kautilyan position that the ends justified the means. And the Kennedy administration tried various ways to eliminate Fidel Castro of Cuba during the Cold War.

It is questionable as to whether Kautilya should be in a book like this one, which examines various systems of ethics. For it is doubtful that Kautilya had any use for ethics as such. As has been said, he was a pragmatist, a propagandist, an egoist, and a realist. What really mattered to him was success, not the intricate dancing around the subject of right and wrong, good and bad, better and best. At the very least, as with Machiavelli, he exemplifies the harsher and darker side of ethics, the flexibility of ethics, the subjectivity of ethics, and the debatable purpose of ethics. His ethics might be thought of as the "ethics of success" or the "ethics of achievable ends." If it is ethics at all, it certainly can be subsumed under the general category of egoistic ethics. Such an ethics may not be embraced by many ethically inclined people today, but it is certainly not alien to actual human activity.

■ ■ ■

Boesche, Roger. 2003. *The First Great Political Realist: Kautilya and His Arthashastra.* Lanham, Md.: Rowman and Littlefield.

Gowen, Herbert H. 1929. "The Indian Machiavelli: Political Theory in India Two Thousand Years Ago." *Political Science Quarterly* 44, no. 2: 173–92.

Palmar, Aradhana. 1987. *Techniques of Statecraft: A Study of Kautilya's Arthashastra.* New Delhi: Atma Ram and Sons.

Ramesh, Jairam. 2002. *Kautilya Today.* New Delhi: India Research Press.

12

Ayn Rand
Rational Self-Interest

JOHN C. MERRILL

Arguably the modern thinker who best represents the egoistic stance in ethics has been the popular writer Ayn Rand (1905–1982), Russian emigrant turned novelist and nonacademic philosopher. Although largely shunned by more liberal professional philosophers, Rand has consistently rallied huge numbers (especially young people) to her individualism, self-enhancement, and rationalism.

Generations of twentieth-century college students were drawn to her strong and clear views of self-esteem, rational self-interest, freedom, honesty, hard work, and integrity. While many of her beliefs seem to reflect elements of existentialism, Ayn Rand was far from an existentialist. She was devoted to reason and had little patience with intuitivism, subjectivism, relativism, and emotion. Rationalism was the foundation of her philosophy.

Today, more than twenty-five years after her death, her novels— all reflecting her philosophy—are still selling well—hundreds of thousands of copies a year. Rand has never been very popular among academic philosophers, but increasingly they are paying more attention to her.[1] However, there is still serious concern among many philosophers about her "too conservative" ideas and her simplification of complex concepts. Asked to summarize her ideas briefly, she answered: "Metaphysics: objective reality. Epistemology: reason. Ethics: self-interest. Politics: capitalism."

A believer in objectivity and scientific certainties, Rand labeled her philosophy "objectivism" and combined her love of rationalism

1. David Glenn, "Advocates of Objectivism Make New Inroads," A8.

with a kind of Aristotelian concept of virtue and self-development. Her novels *The Fountainhead* and *Atlas Shrugged* and her many nonfiction books on philosophy (e.g., *For the New Intellectual* [1961] and *The Virtue of Selfishness* [1964]) illustrate her morality of rational self-interest. Any form of collectivism or community-led morality was anathema to her and she constantly emphasized egocentric motivation, meritocracy (rewarding excellence), and freedom in the communication arena. She condemned as irrational and immoral the ideas of any brand of collectivism and altruism. Often in opposition to establishment philosophers, Rand saw them as promoting statism in political philosophy, subjectivism in epistemology, and relativism, mysticism, and emotionalism in ethics.

Ayn Rand's ethical philosophy resonates to some degree with that of Erich Fromm, Aldous Huxley, and Ortega y Gasset in its belief that some values are better than others and all opinions are not equal; there are objective distinctions. A person should be guided by intellect, not by urges, wishes, and whims—everyone who lives by independent judgment and self-esteem. Of all the virtues, for Rand, rationality is basic. Her emphasis, as she writes in *The Virtue of Selfishness,* is on a person's "full, conscious awareness" and "a commitment to the fullest perception of reality within one's power" (1965, 25–30). She sounds a lot like Bertrand Russell, who maintained that rational people always consider their own self-interest of the greatest importance. Russell believed that it is seldom in a person's interest to do anything that is harmful to others. Rand would agree with that.

She pulled no punches in her criticism of modern culture, which she saw as having too little respect for values and reason and peopled largely by those who are guided by feelings, instincts, wishes, whims, and revelations. She scorned the person who, like a zombie, rallied to every call of the collective, and viewed conforming to the group as an unethical thing to do (1961, 50).

Rand, in her objectivist philosophy, gave special attention to reason. Her "new intellectual" is a person who is intellect-directed, for rationality is the fountain of all virtues. Reason, the only source of knowledge for Rand, serves as a guide to values and action. She shows an affinity with Immanuel Kant in that her objectivist ethics stresses that one's life is an end in itself. With Kant she believed that every person is an end, not a means to an end set by others. But she disagreed with Kant in his belief that we cannot be certain about the true nature of reality. This did not fit her objectivist philosophy.

Nor would she have much in common with the twenty-first-century postmodernists and their relativism and denial of objectivity.

Rand's emphasis on selfishness is not inconsistent with humanism, although it is often considered so. The basic social principle of her ethics is that all human beings are ends and must live for their own selves, neither sacrificing themselves to others nor sacrificing others to themselves. So we can see that her philosophy has consideration for others and their individual worth and freedom, and at the same time celebrates self-interest and self-esteem. In fact, for Rand, the ethical person cannot deny his or her worth as an actor; it is because of this that others can be treated with respect and dignity. Pride, real legitimate pride, for Rand, does not go before a fall. It is a valuable asset and, as she wrote in *Atlas Shrugged,* it is the "recognition of the fact that you are your own highest value and, like all of man's values, it has to be earned" (1957, 35).

For Rand, self-interest is the motivation for ethics. The moral person is not the one who sacrifices or forsakes life; rather it is the person who creates and makes life possible. The human life is the moral standard for Rand. The person's life is the moral standard, and one lives for his or her own sake and never sacrifices self to others or others to self. Live and let live. Be happy and let others be happy. This, for Rand, was the purpose of morality.

The idea that people should be treated as equals was, for Rand, ridiculous. People are not equal, and the very idea of egalitarianism interlocked with some kind of democratic idealism was not only impossible but harmful to human growth and progress. Merit and its encouragement is what is needed. Competition is the spark that ignites a vital and forward-looking society. It is the outstanding figures, the thinking and acting members of society, who push civilization forward. Excel, win, succeed, work hard, prize self, be authentic, love freedom, and accept personal responsibility. This is the essence of Rand's ethical—and pragmatic—philosophy. It is an ethical philosophy of rational self-interest and it is the idea of "rational" that keeps the self-interest from deteriorating into harmful and negative egocentrism that eliminates all social concern.

Let us summarize a few of the foundational ideas in Ayn Rand's ethics:

* rationality (commitment to perceive reality to the best of our ability)

* independence (relying on our own judgment and acceptance of responsibility for our actions)
* justice (identifying people for what they are and treating them accordingly)
* productivity (bringing knowledge, goods, or services into existence)
* pride (dedication to achieving the highest potential in our character and life without self-sacrifice)
* integrity (acting according to the judgment of our consciousness)
* honesty (never seeking values by faking reality)

An evil or unethical society, for Rand, comes about through individuals closing their eyes to it, doing nothing to prevent it, and thus in reality condoning it. She wrote in 1957 that the "evil of the world is made possible by nothing but the sanction you give it." And again referring to evil a few years later, she wrote that the spread of evil "is the symptom of a vacuum," and that whenever evil wins, it is "only by default"—by what she called "the moral failure of those who evade the fact that there can be no compromise on basic principles."

What is the kernel of Randian ethics or what does morality demand from us? Her answer: to struggle to the best of our ability to do good and avoid doing evil consciously. If we do that, Rand would regard us as completely good—if we never do evil deliberately. In the area of communication, Rand would realize that a discussant sometimes becomes angry and speaks or acts in a way that gives offense. This person should later (or immediately) recognize the mistake, and make apologies or amends. And, what's more, the person should be proud of having the maturity and courage to do so.

Aristotle probably made the deepest impression on Rand, even during her early college days in Russia. His metaphysics of objective reality and his concept of individual worth helped in the formation of her philosophy. Like Aristotle, Rand believed that an objective reality exists independent of the mind and is capable of being known. Even her ethics reflected Aristotle's to a certain degree: a person needs a system of moral guidelines to live successfully and flourish as a human being.

Another philosopher influencing Rand's thinking was Friedrich Nietzsche, who instilled in her the reverence for human potential, the heroic, a deep suspicion of altruism, and a firm opposition to collectivism. Although she had some disagreement with Nietzsche, she generally came to terms with him and in her introduction of the twenty-fifth anniversary edition of *The Fountainhead* she concluded with his statement that "the noble soul has reverence for itself" (1943).

Also along with Nietzsche, she had little respect for Immanuel Kant's "duty" ethics that, for her, enthroned selflessness and the devaluation of personal goals as moral benefits. For Kant, acting from duty and only from duty was ethical, whereas Rand saw this inflexible, formalistic, impersonal ethics as resulting in self-sacrifice.

The teleological stance in ethics, especially the utilitarian variety, got little respect from Rand, because of its altruistic emphasis. One of the few writers who has seriously opposed an altruistic stance, she has championed an ethics of "self-first" and has argued tirelessly for what she calls "rational self interest." As she writes in *The Virtue of Selfishness,* altruism is responsible, more than anything else, for the "the arrested moral development of mankind" (1964, 68).

Modern communicators should not be reluctant to criticize or to be politically incorrect. And she would urge them not to hesitate to judge. Rand would take Christ's injunction to "judge not" and make it read "judge and be prepared to be judged." Rand, like Nietzsche, saw religion as making people weak, timid, and group-minded instead of stressing personal growth and happiness. She would have little sympathy with the communitarians of today who, she would say, promote their goal of social stability and egalitarianism at the expense of personal worth and growth.

Ayn Rand disdained mysticism and intuitionism. She reacted against thinkers like the German Arthur Schopenhauer, perhaps the West's foremost intuitionist, who had little faith in rationalism and believed that a kind of instinctual morality based on Hindu mysticism was superior to other moralities. He was basically religious and poetic rather than prosaic and scientific. At least he mistrusted reason and enthroned feeling. And whereas Rand would exalt the will, Schopenhauer thought it should be subdued so that the transcendental world of aesthetic appreciation could be realized.

In one way Rand and Schopenhauer were similar. They would both seek happiness within the individual self rather than relying on others to make them happy. Both thinkers would be unconcerned with altruistic activity—but Rand would empower the ego and enhance personal striving whereas Schopenhauer would attempt to eliminate the ego so our restless pursuits are stilled and our desires are washed away. Rand would try to transcend the world and Schopenhauer would try to be one with the world, a kind of Oriental position.

The journalist and other public communicators have a responsibility to formulate clear, direct messages, to provide an objective view of the world around them, and to refrain from self-denying and hypocritical messages. For Rand, communication should accentuate, even glorify, the individual person and his or her potential value and creativity.

Although the individual person held a high place in existentialism, Ayn Rand had little use for that philosophy mainly because of its emphasis on emotion and instinct and its insistence that objectivity did not exist. Kierkegaard, one of the founders of modern existentialism, for example, denied any such thing as an impartial observer, believing instead that all truth is filtered through a subjective, psychological strainer. For Kierkegaard, a person could not step outside oneself and become a dispassionate, neutral observer. Rand tended to agree more with philosophers like the Frenchman Descartes (1596–1650) who said that passions, intuitions, and imagination are barriers to truth. He, like Rand, had more faith in objectivity and science, built on a rational philosophy.

Basically Ayn Rand was a proponent of peaceful relationships. Not really a pacifist (she believed that self-defense was morally correct), she did, however, oppose American involvement in both world wars, the Korean War, the Vietnam War, and undoubtedly she would have opposed the U.S. invasion of Middle Eastern countries. She said of Vietnam that it represented the ultimate suicidal extreme of altruism on a global scale where American soldiers were being killed for no real purpose. She certainly would have said the same thing later about the war in Iraq.

The modern communicator might find Rand's ideas and writing style useful in implanting ideas and information in a direct and forceful way. Capitalism being the main foundation of American mass communication, her dedication to individualistic egoistic ethics should find acceptance with most mass communicators. Competition and self-respect, along with the following of rational tenets, have an important place in communication ethics. Underneath protestations of public service, concern for others, and altruism lies a strong Randian self-love and egoistic motivation.

The modern communicator will surely find Rand's dedication to freedom of expression refreshing. This indicates her basic and abiding faith in the Enlightenment and its emphasis on honest and liberating dialogue. She was especially supportive of the individual vis-à-vis the state and the person threatened by institutional slavery. In short, she believed in freedom from any type of intellectual conformity. Such freedom, for her, was absolutely necessary for any consideration of ethics. For her, individual freedom trumps so-called rights. For example, such a concept as the "people's right to know" would place an obligation on communicators which they, in their freedom, should not have. Choice is necessary in communication ethics, and "rights" of receivers negates the communicator's choice (1964, 87–90).

Learn to value yourself, Rand has advised, and fight for your happiness. Be proud; recognize that you are your own highest value. Be rational and ethics will take care of itself. Don't scorn money; it is through money that we deal with one another and without it men become tools of others, she writes in *Atlas Shrugged*. "Blood, whips and guns—or dollars. Take your choice—there is no other." Happiness and good ethics, she believes, are derived from using reason, echoing A. L. Whitehead when he writes in *The Function of Reason* that the "very function of Reason is to promote the art of life."[2]

Ayn Rand's philosophy, for many communicators, will seem too harsh and its selfish emphasis will alienate many who wish to participate in dialogue on an equal basis with other communicants. Her moral philosophy is stern and self-centered and devoid of any desire to conform to the dictates of the social group. But she is convinced that when one follows his or her own light, the path through the difficult moral morass will be properly illuminated. If one is not careful, Rand would say, in the name of altruism this light will be lost, and the resulting darkness will eliminate all but conformist ethics.

■ ■ ■

Glenn, David. 2007. "Advocates of Objectivism Make New Inroads." *Chronicle of Higher Education*, July 13, 2007.

Rand, Ayn. 1943. *The Fountainhead*. Indianapolis: Bobbs Merrill.

———. 1957. *Atlas Shrugged*. New York: Random House.

———. 1961. *For the New Intellectual*. New York: Random House, Signet.

———. 1964. *The Virtue of Selfishness: A New Concept of Egoism*. New York: New American Library, Signet Books.

Whitehead, Alfred N. 1929. *The Function of Reason*. Boston: Beacon.

2. Alfred N. Whitehead, *The Function of Reason*.

The Autonomy Stance
Loyalty to Freedom

In the autonomy stance, ethicists are freedom-lovers first of all.

They resist especially the rule-bound ethics of the historical figures examined in Part IV. Similar in some ways to the egoistic ethicists described in Part II, the thinkers in Part III place a high value on freely determined ethical choices, even when it means choosing to be a social nonconformist.

For John Locke, freedom was a natural right that societies should protect and promote at all costs. Henry David Thoreau did not believe in irresponsible freedom, but insisted on liberty from undue government restraints. Dietrich Bonhoeffer, from a deep commitment to his own integrity, refused to compromise with political authorities. For Hannah Arendt also, ethics requires maximum freedom, and Paulo Freire promotes emancipation from the oppressors who restrain ordinary human beings within a culture of silence.

PART III

Henry David Thoreau
Value of Solitude

STEPHANIE CRAFT

People tend to know two things about Henry David Thoreau, if they know anything about him at all: First, he lived in a small cabin near Walden Pond, hoping that in simplifying his life he would be able to truly and fully experience it. Second, he once went to jail for refusing to pay his poll tax, an instance of protest he described in his highly influential essay on civil disobedience.

At least one biographer of Thoreau lamented that in knowing only those two things, the "man in the street . . . has a vague notion that he spent one half of his life doing the one and the other half the other."[1]

In fact, Thoreau's entire life—not just the two years on Walden Pond or the night in jail—was his work. In *Walden,* Thoreau declared: "Our whole life is startlingly moral" (2004, 210). He lived his philosophy through keen and disciplined observation, self-improvement and self-reliance, practicality and fierce autonomy and recorded it in his published works, which never earned him a living, and his personal journals, which at his death contained some two million words. Gifted leaders and artists from Mohandas Gandhi and Frank Lloyd Wright to Martin Luther King, Jr., and Sinclair Lewis cite Thoreau as an inspiration. But for generations, Thoreau's legacy lived in the shadows of his nineteenth-century contemporaries.

It is, perhaps, cliché to remark on an artist's being unappreciated in his own time or in ours. It is true, however, that Thoreau's relationship to the New England Transcendentalists is somewhat misunderstood,

1. Walter Harding, *The Days of Henry David Thoreau.*

that critical attention paid to his mentor Ralph Waldo Emerson often obscured Thoreau's unique contributions to literature and philosophy, and that current mainstream philosophy is still attempting to determine whether and where he belongs. Even so, Thoreau's "ethics of perception,"[2] his views on individualism and the pursuit of truth, and his attitudes toward writing offer journalists rich insights into the nature of knowledge that have broad implications for how they see and report on the world.

Thoreau's world consisted largely of the area in and around Concord, Massachusetts, where he was born David Henry Thoreau in 1817 and died of tuberculosis in 1862. (His parents called him by his middle name. He later began using his first and middle names inverted, which probably served only to enhance his reputation around Concord as something of an eccentric.) As a child, Thoreau enjoyed a "hardy outdoor life" in the woods, meadows, and streams around Concord.[3] The scholarly one of the four Thoreau children, Henry went to Harvard in 1833. His coursework, as was typical of the time, focused on Greek, Latin, history, mathematics, English, philosophy, natural history, and foreign language. A good student, Thoreau nonetheless seems to have played down the importance of college after his graduation in 1837. Still, biographers credit his exposure in college to the Scottish "common sense" philosophers (e.g., Reid, Stewart, Brown), who questioned John Locke's theory of knowledge, with laying the groundwork for Thoreau's and others' transcendentalist ideas.[4]

Thoreau moved back to Concord and the outdoors he loved after graduating from Harvard. At various times, he worked as a teacher, a pencil maker in his father's factory, a land surveyor, and a handyman. He also grew vegetables. He never married, though he is believed to have been in love twice and to have once suffered the embarrassment of a rather unprecedented and unwanted proposal from a woman older than he. Thoreau had close friends and family, intimate connections that are difficult to square with the descriptions of his personality as cold, remote, exacting, and overly sensitive. People seem to have regarded him as a singular personality, a kind of force of the nature he spent his life describing.

2. Rick Anthony Furtak, "Henry David Thoreau."
3. Henry S. Salt, *Life of Henry David Thoreau,* 6.
4. Harding, *The Days of Henry David Thoreau.*

Meeting Emerson was the pivotal moment of Thoreau's life. The introduction was brought about in 1837 by Emerson's sister-in-law, who had heard from Thoreau's sister Helen that a passage in Thoreau's journal echoed ideas Emerson had discussed in one of his lectures.[5] Thoreau's subsequent visit to Emerson, at Emerson's request, marked the beginning of a lifelong friendship and intellectual discourse. Along with Bronson Alcott, Margaret Fuller, George Ripley, and others, Emerson had formed a circle of thinkers drawn to the idea that the human mind transcends experience. The New England Transcendentalists, as they were known, came to transcendentalism by way of the English Romantics—chiefly Samuel Taylor Coleridge and Thomas Carlyle—who were themselves steeped in German Idealism. Transcendentalism was New England's version of Romanticism,[6] complete with its characteristic self-preoccupation and emphasis on man's relationship to nature, and with elements of Unitarianism's reaction against Calvinism's bleak view of humanity added to the mix.[7]

Transcendentalism derives, roughly, from Immanuel Kant's ideas regarding the power and authority of the human mind in determining how we know the world. In particular, Kant claimed that how we experience life is conditioned on certain facts we can learn only upon reflection—that is, they aren't directly accessible by our senses. The immense importance of Emerson in particular, and the transcendentalists in general, on Thoreau's work is undisputed, even though Thoreau came to disagree sharply with them on a number of issues, including the route to truth transcendentalism suggests. In many ways, Thoreau's practicality set him apart.

Indeed, scholars agree that Thoreau did not wear the mantle of New England transcendentalism well. His ideas might, in fact, be closer than theirs to Kant's transcendental idealism.[8] Thoreau did not share the religious bent of Emerson's circle, disputed the notion that man holds dominion over nature, and did not agree with their contention that one's senses are unreliable as evidence. While claiming no particular philosophy for himself, Thoreau took the transcendentalist project in a very practical direction. Henry S. Salt describes this in terms of two sides to Thoreau's character: the transcendental

5. Salt, *Life of Thoreau,* 23.
6. Michael Cisco, "Henry David Thoreau: Bachelor of Thought and Nature," 60.
7. Furtak, "Thoreau."
8. Ibid.

side, focused on the possibilities of the human mind, and the practical side, focused on the realities of the world.[9] It is in this combination that Thoreau's importance to journalists might be discovered.

Thoreau's practical side is nowhere more evident than in the two years and two months he spent at Walden Pond. He set off on Independence Day of 1845 to the ten-by-fifteen-foot hut he had built about a mile and a half from Concord on property Emerson owned. His purpose: to seek knowledge and truth.

> I went to the woods because I wished to live deliberately, to front only the essential facts of life, and see if I could learn what it had to teach, and not, when I came to die, discover that I had not lived. I did not wish to live what was not life, living is so dear; nor did I wish to practice resignation, unless it was quite necessary. I wanted to live deep and suck out all the marrow of life, to live so sturdily and Spartan-like as to put to rout all that was not life, to cut a broad swath and shave close, to drive life into a corner, and reduce it to its lowest terms, and, if it proved to be mean, why then to get the whole and genuine meanness of it, and publish its meanness to the world; or if it were sublime, to know it by experience, and be able to give a true account of it in my next excursion. (2004, 88)

What was so practical about seeking knowledge in nature? Thoreau was not content to merely muse about the truths the natural world might hold. He set out to examine and experience that world as closely as possible, to get his hands on it, free of the distractions of social life. In fact, he believed an individual must be separate from society to find truth. During his two-year "experiment" in radical simplicity at Walden Pond, Thoreau spent most of his time alone, carefully recording the details of the natural beauty around him, his daily rituals and routines, and his views on both. He received the occasional guest, though he wrote that he preferred the guests who came while he was out.

On the surface, Thoreau's exile in the woods had something in common with the utopian communities that sprang up in the mid nineteenth century, two of which (Brook Farm and Fruitlands) had been started by his friends. Unlike these communities, however,

---

9. Salt, *Life of Thoreau*, 102.

Thoreau did not seek to improve society by improving the circumstances of community. His was a project of intense individualism, an attempt to understand an individual's obligation to himself and not just to society. One biographer summarizes the perspective this way: "An individual who does not know himself, his own worth, and his own freedom, may not cooperate freely."[10] In Thoreau's view, self-improvement was the necessary precursor to societal improvement.

Journalists may appreciate this individualist attitude—expressed in *Walden* as well as in "Civil Disobedience"—because it has the libertarian texture of much of American press theory emphasizing a watchdog press that supports self-governance. Thoreau's views on the relationship between the individual and the state and on the importance of following one's conscience were published in 1849 in the essay "Resistance to Civil Government," later renamed "Civil Disobedience." Opposed to slavery, Thoreau had stopped paying his poll tax as a form of protest. He was arrested in 1846 and spent a night in jail before someone (it's unclear just who) paid the tax for him and he was freed, much to his displeasure. In "Civil Disobedience," Thoreau wrote, "There will never be a really free and enlightened State until the State comes to recognize the individual as a higher and independent power, from which all its own power and authority are derived, and treats him accordingly."

The view that the law of conscience is higher than civil law is in line with transcendentalist thinking. By refusing to pay the tax, Thoreau put that view into action. His transcendental side, as Salt called it, also is reflected in how he understood the character of knowledge and truth. If our whole lives are moral, as Thoreau proclaimed in *Walden,* then our perceptions, our ways of seeking knowledge and truth, must have moral dimensions. Thoreau, in some sense, posits an "ethics of perception" in which the observer may be called to account for what, and how well, he perceives.[11] Thoreau himself spent his days in observation of nature, honing his perceptual abilities. "The perception of beauty," he wrote, "is a moral test" (*Journal,* June 21, 1852). The connection to journalism is easy to make: Journalists, who also seek truth, bear moral responsibility for what they cover and how. But the fact of such responsibility is hardly a revelation. Thoreau pushes the point further, suggesting an understanding of

10. Cisco, "Thoreau: Bachelor of Thought and Nature," 77.
11. Furtak, "Thoreau."

truth that might seem at first glance to be at odds with the view of many contemporary journalists, not to mention their audiences.

Truth, in Thoreau's view, is subjective. His quest to see things as they really are involved careful, diligent, even laborious observation. But Thoreau did not consider his observations to have an objective quality to them, as though his quest was concerned with the discovery of mere "facts." Rather, he considered the observer to be inseparable from what he observes. Who we are acts as a lens on what we see. In that way, subjectivity is not a barrier to truth, but a means of accessing it. In making this claim, Thoreau was trying to bridge the gap between science and art, to recognize that each approach to knowledge is incomplete on its own.

That the observer and observed are bound so tightly together in Thoreau's way of thinking has at least one important implication for the professional communicator. Our perceptions are limited not only by what is available for us to see and by our ability to see, but also by what we value—toward what do we turn our attention? In arguing that we see only what concerns us, Thoreau points again to the moral character of the choices (journalistic and otherwise) we make. As Alfred I. Tauber notes, the fact that knowledge depends on an individual's ability to see means "the world as known is thus radically dependent on character."[12]

In other hands, the account of the Walden experiment might have read as part lab journal and part grocery list. In Thoreau's hands, it became one of the most important works in American literature. We cannot know, of course, whether its success would have surprised Thoreau. But in his own time he was not entirely hopeful about his— or anyone's—ability to communicate ideas to others. That Thoreau valued firsthand accounts is clear; not only his journals, but all his work was personal. In *Walden* he asks for the same authenticity from others: "I, on my side, require of every writer, first or last, a simple and sincere account of his own life, and not merely what he has heard of other men's lives" (2004, 2). Even so, his ideas about the nature of knowledge seem to suggest that any such account of another's life, because it would be mediated by the process of writing it, would be unable to convey the full reality of what one has experienced. The written account is distinct from what it describes. Perhaps, Thoreau

12. Alfred I. Tauber, *Henry David Thoreau and the Moral Agency of Knowing*, 4–5.

wrote, "the facts most astounding and most real are never communicated by man to man" (2004, 208).

These words foreshadow the concerns about the gap between "the world outside and the pictures in our heads" that journalist Walter Lippmann famously raised in his book *Public Opinion* some sixty years later. Lippmann worried that our knowledge of the world was inescapably skewed and that in a world of imperfect knowledge, the prospects for journalism and democracy were dim. But one need not read Thoreau's work as suggesting that attempts at communication are futile. Just the opposite is true. Communicating ideas may be difficult, but Thoreau spent his life making the effort. In doing so, and in his unwavering commitment to uncovering truth and to individual responsibility, Thoreau offers high standards to which journalists can aspire.

■   ■   ■

Cisco, Michael. 1987. "Henry David Thoreau: Bachelor of Thought and Nature." In *Henry David Thoreau*, edited by Harold Bloom. Philadelphia: Chelsea House.

Furtak, Rick Anthony. 2006. "Henry David Thoreau." In *The Stanford Encyclopedia of Philosophy*, edited by Edward N. Zalta. Fall 2006 ed. http://plato.stanford.edu/archives/fall2006/entries/thoreau.

Goodman, Russell. 2007. "Transcendentalism." In *The Stanford Encyclopedia of Philosophy*, edited by Edward N. Zalta. Spring 2007 ed. http://plato.stanford.edu/archives/spr2007/entries/transcendentalism.

Harding, Walter. 1965. *The Days of Henry Thoreau*. New York: Alfred A. Knopf.

Salt, Henry S. 1993. *Life of Henry David Thoreau*. Urbana: University of Illinois Press. Original work published in 1890.

Tauber, Alfred I. 2001. *Henry David Thoreau and the Moral Agency of Knowing*. Berkeley: University of California Press.

Thoreau, Henry David. 1962. *The Journal of Henry D. Thoreau*. Edited by Bradford Torrey and Francis H. Allen. New York: Dover Books. Original work published in 1906.

———. 2004. *Walden: A Fully Annotated Edition*. Edited by Jeffrey S. Cramer. New Haven, Conn.: Yale University Press.

———. 2004. *Walden or Life in the Woods* and *On the Duty of Civil Disobedience*. Edited by W. S. Merwin and Perry Miller. New York: Penguin Group.

———. 1973. *The Writings of Henry D. Thoreau: Reform Papers*. Edited by Wendell Glick. Princeton, N.J.: Princeton University Press.

14

John Locke
Natural Rights

PATRICK LEE PLAISANCE

John Locke was born into a Puritan family in Somerset, England, in 1632—the year Galileo published his *Dialogue Concerning the Two Chief World Systems.* Due to family connections through his father's involvement in the civil war over the claim of Charles I to the throne, Locke began studying at Christ Church in Oxford in the early 1660s, but was dissatisfied with the Aristotelian paradigm of knowledge that still dominated at the time. He pursued a lifelong interest in medicine, befriending Robert Boyle, one of the great scientists of the age. In 1666, Locke met a man named Anthony Ashley Cooper, who would later become the first Earl of Shaftesbury. The relationship developed into one of the most important and influential in Locke's life. As his adviser and personal physician, Locke directed a medical procedure that saved Shaftesbury's life, and the aristocrat's involvement in efforts to block the policies of Charles II drew Locke into the center of English politics. As a result, Locke's more illiberal early positions from his time at Oxford (disdain for religious tolerance and skepticism toward the role of popular consent in government) shifted toward the more "Lockean" positions of religious tolerance and freedom constrained by moral imperatives that we are familiar with today.

Locke's connection with Shaftesbury, who was eventually imprisoned in the Tower of London and later exiled to Holland for his anti-Catholic opposition to Charles, caused trouble for the philosopher as well. Locke relocated to France and later to Holland. After several years abroad, Locke returned to England upon the enthroning of the Protestant monarchs William and Mary in 1689. Shortly afterward, he published many of his landmark works setting forth his arguments against absolute power and in defense of individual rights. He remained active in politics for the rest of his life, serving as a trade official, which involved him in the affairs of the English colonies. His final years were devoted largely to writing on religious subjects, including a commentary on the epistles of St. Paul. He died in 1704. He never married, and as far as historians know, never fathered children.

Locke was defined by the turbulent moment in history in which he found himself. He straddled the medieval and postmodern worlds, and had feet metaphorically planted in the age of faith as well as the age of skepticism and empiricism. His religion and his politics were intertwined: his religious convictions were "deep, idiosyncratic, unsentimental, decidedly Protestant and staunchly anti-Catholic,"[1] which in turn informed what later became his central themes of skepticism of authority and a vision of freedom explicitly constrained by certain moral and rational boundaries. Few Enlightenment thinkers have so deeply influenced the modern world or have shaped our understanding of liberty as Locke; indeed, the indebtedness of America's "founding fathers" to his writings set the stage for the United States to develop into the most "Lockean" of nations. He was unquestioningly empiricist and individualist, yet simultaneously insistent that the "rights" of man to liberty and the fruits of his labors had a theological foundation—that these rights must be understood as explicitly God-given. Locke is thus a prominent "natural rights" theorist: he claims, most prominently in his *Second Treatise of Government* of 1689, that the rights to liberty and property that we claim to have are in a sense "natural" to us, inherent in the human condition rather than stemming from society or some authority. Locke's *Second Treatise* sets forth his trademark justification for private property ownership and, more generally, the natural right to liberty and possessions: "[E]very man has a property in his own person: this nobody has any right to but himself," Locke wrote. As a result, "the labour of [a person's] body, and the work of his hands, we may say, are properly his," so that "whatsoever then he removes out of the state that nature hath provided, and left it in, he hath mixed his own labour with, and joined to it something that is his own, and thereby makes it his property" (1689/2003, II, 27).

1. E. Feser, *Locke*, 7.

It is his position at a critical crossroads in Western history that drives his claims and his perceptions—a man with Puritan roots who came to embody the ideals of secular liberty in the age of reason. Locke is a hero to many contemporary conservatives for his libertarian framework, yet others have claimed Locke should be credited as a pro-tofeminist because of his attacks on the assumptions of patriarchy.[2] It should be no surprise, then, why Locke has retained such an honored place in American political theory. Thomas Jefferson's Declaration of Independence is a direct importation, with a few deviations, of Locke's political philosophy. Nor should it be a surprise why he remains such a subject of controversy and criticism—the sweep of his polemics that constitutes one of his attributes also serves as the source of key problems and weaknesses of his theoretical work.

Locke has long been a hero of libertarians who emphasize the importance of limited government and individual rights and who express supreme confidence in "the marketplace of ideas" to deliver the "truth" in deliberating important public policy decisions. Applied to communication ethics, Locke provides a philosophical basis for autonomous agency as a prime, if not absolute, value to ensure the vibrancy and validity of that marketplace. Any perceived restraint on the ability of journalists to report on the news, including self-censorship, undermines the democratic enterprise, according to this Lockean framework. Professional communicators must be given maximum latitude, and must be trusted to be guided by their own internal moral imperatives, if they are to properly carry out their public service functions.

It is important to understand what exactly Locke was reacting *against* in much of his writings. Locke is among the key thinkers of the early period of modern philosophy who abandoned the Aristotelian and Thomist worldviews that so dominated medieval Europe. In short, Aristotle claimed that we "know" the existence of things both through their "substance"—their independent makeup and organizational structure—and their "attributes"—features tied to the thing that has them. A blue ball, for example, is a substance, but the blueness and roundness of the ball are not, since these attributes exist only in the ball itself. This approach to knowledge leads to questions and claims about the final "causes" or origins of things, which, for

---

2. M. A. Butler, "Early Liberal Roots of Feminism: John Locke's Attack on Patriarchy."

St. Augustine and Thomas Aquinas, raised critical questions about the basis for the belief in God and about human nature. Aristotle's claim that things only exist through their substance and attributes posed serious challenges to Christian claims about the existence of the human soul and God's hand in the world. Aristotle claimed that a thing can lose its "form" but the "form" itself is something that exists independently from any actual thing. For example, a triangle drawn on a blackboard might be partially erased, thus removing the triangle "form" from the drawn image, but that does not affect the reality of "triangleness." Analogously, a human body may lose its soul upon death, but the soul, since it is a "form," does not perish. But Christian theologians then faced a problem: if the human soul, as an Aristotelian "form," were immortal merely in the sense that the form of a triangle is, there is no guarantee of *personal* immortality, only of the general *idea* of immortality itself. Aquinas, in response, claimed that the human soul is unique among all forms in that while it was associated with the body, it did not fully depend on the body in the way all other forms depended on the things of which they were a feature. Another part of this uniqueness was that it exhibited natural ends or purposes, which for theologians meant the pursuit of the "good" and, ultimately, eternal communion with God. Thus, understanding these ends results in knowledge of what we are morally obliged to do for the realization of those ends and what defines the good. This Thomist system of morality came to be known as "natural law." Aquinas said that God "directs" things to certain ends, but does not have a hand in the specific content those ends might take.

Locke had many aims of his medieval predecessors. He wanted to demonstrate the existence of God and to prove a theory of natural rights. But at the same time, he rejected the Augustinian claims of causality and natural ends. His efforts rested on Descartes' rationalism that rejected claims of final causes and purposes on which Aristotelian theology was based: it is only through reasoning proceeding from innate ideas that genuine knowledge of anything stems, Descartes argued. Locke went only so far in agreeing with Descartes, opposing Descartes' claim about innate ideas as likely to lead to dogmatism and the stifling of individual thought. But Locke embraced his rationalism that reconstructed knowledge on the basis of what the individual mind could discover for itself. For Locke, this rationalist framework reaffirmed his own skepticism of authority and tradition. Locke claimed that individuals are governed by natural law, but he sought to make his case, most notably in his *Essay Concerning Human Understanding* (1690), without resorting to the Thomistic understanding of natural law based on final causes that "proved" the existence of God's hand in human affairs. Rather, he appealed to the idea that humans are equals by virtue of each being creatures of the same God. Thus, Locke sought to stake out a position between medieval dogmatism and secular skepticism in his project to privilege freedom and autonomy, but in a way that borrowed from both frameworks. This project produces a tension that threatens to undermine his central claim of the right to individual freedom within identified boundaries. As Feser summarizes: "Lockeanism seems pulled in two directions: rightward, back toward the medieval tradition he rejected, with its more robust theology and communitarianism; and leftward, toward the hyper-individualism, secularism and skepticism of the contemporary world."[3]

Among Locke's most enduring contributions, even as they have exposed the anti-Catholic Locke to criticisms of hypocrisy, are his efforts to provide a philosophical justification for religious tolerance. If real knowledge is nearly impossible due to the limits of reason and experience, then toleration, Locke suggests in his *Essay,* is the only rational policy in an era of violent political and religious disputes. This is one reason why Locke remains such a central figure in contemporary politics.

Critics of Locke's libertarian framework have long argued that it is oversimplistic in its approach to liberty and that it fails to adequately reflect the inherently *social* roots of human identity and existence. Locke also has been criticized for misinterpreting or misrepresenting claims of medieval theologians in his attempt to replace their explanation of knowledge with his own. Locke also fails in important ways, critics claim, to address the dilemmas of social and political inequality, particularly the contemporary manifestations of each. "[N]early all of Locke's specific teachings have ceased to be directly relevant to our times," suggested Thomas Cook. "They have become theoretically indefensible and socially irrelevant" (Locke 1689/1947, p. xxxviii). Feminist theorists such as Seyla Benhabib have claimed that Locke's theologically grounded framework of rights only serves to reinforce patriarchal power and devalue attributes of empathy, support, and collaboration commonly associated with the domestic—

3. Feser, *Locke,* 28.

i.e., "feminine"—sphere.[4] Stephen Newman and others question the use of a Lockean market economy paradigm to represent the sum of human interaction and social life, including politics.[5] Feser concluded that contradictions in Locke's writings require that "those who seek to appropriate Locke's legacy today must decide which part they value most, for they cannot coherently have it all. . . . It is no longer possible (if it ever was) to be a Lockean."[6] These criticisms hold important implications for how Locke's libertarianism might be successfully applied to communication ethics. The vision of a defiantly independent, fearless, and intrepid journalist uncovering the unvarnished "truth" for the public is certainly appealing on one level, but is hard to square either with an interactive journalism that seeks to engage and reflect society or with the reality of the professional journalist who is constrained by a galaxy of ideological, extramedia, and economic forces.

And yet Locke never lets us marginalize or make light of the centrality of freedom and the imperatives of carrying out our roles as moral autonomous agents. Whichever holes or weaknesses we may seek in his theology, and however we may fault his lack of originality or precision, he articulated better and earlier than most several intertwined strands of thought that have come to embody modern Western life as we know it: individual rights, empiricism, skepticism of authority, religious minimalism, and consent of the governed.

■　■　■

Benhabib, Seyla. 1992. *Situating the Self: Gender, Community and Postmodernism in Contemporary Ethics*. London: Routledge.

Butler, M. A. 2007. "Early Liberal Roots of Feminism: John Locke's Attack on Patriarchy." In N. J. Hirschmann and K. M. McClure, eds., *Feminist Interpretations of John Locke*. University Park: Pennsylvania State University Press.

Feser, E. 2007. *Locke*. Oxford, UK: Oneworld Publications.

4. Seyla Benhabib, *Situating the Self: Gender, Community and Postmodernism in Contemporary Ethics*, 153–58.

5. Steven Newman, *Liberalism at Wit's End: The Libertarian Revolt against the Modern State*, preface, chapters 3, 6.

6. Feser, *Locke,* 172.v

Locke, John. 1947. *Two Treatises of Government.* Edited by T. L. Cook. New York: Hafner. Original work published in 1689.

———. 2003. *Two Treatises of Government and a Letter Concerning Toleration.* Edited by I. Shapiro. New Haven, Conn.: Yale University Press. Original work published in 1689.

Newman, Steven L. 1984. *Liberalism at Wit's End: The Libertarian Revolt against the Modern State.* Ithaca, N.Y.: Cornell University Press.

15

Dietrich Bonhoeffer
Courage versus Authority

RONALD C. ARNETT

Introducing Dietrich Bonhoeffer to the field of communication rests upon one key assertion—Bonhoeffer's life and work provide us with insight into a communication style that is responsive to diverse ideas in a time of crisis. His communicative manner is dissimilar from that of those who contend with one another from a standpoint of conviction while being oblivious to the pragmatic importance of self-doubt. Bonhoeffer's position takes us far beyond the impulse of blind defense of one's own ideas, revealing the pragmatic importance of unifying what, at first blush, look like contradictory communicative actions: conviction and doubt. Bonhoeffer's communicative wisdom did not permit him to succumb to the temptation of conviction without question; he tempered his own and others' enthusiasm for assuming the undisputed correctness of their convictions.

To outline Bonhoeffer's contribution to communication, the following sections illuminate the "who," the "what," and the "why" of his contribution. In an era of Nazi tyranny, Bonhoeffer pointed toward "a world come of age" that requires our full communicative participation in shaping societal outcomes. He united doubt and conviction in order to meet the dilemmas of an era defined by disagreement, or what is now termed in postmodern language as narrative and virtue contention. Bonhoeffer offers a communicative model for meeting the demands of an increasingly contentious era. He lives with conviction, knowing the limits of his own position. But one cannot look to Bonhoeffer for "the" answer; he would reject such an impulse out of hand. The value of Bonhoeffer's project is his guidance in suggesting how the interplay of conviction and doubt can assist in navigating the uncertain, intemperate, and dangerous waters of a demanding world.

Who: Dietrich Bonhoeffer

Dietrich Bonhoeffer was born in 1906 in Breslau, Germany. He had a twin sister, Sabina, and six other brothers and sisters. His family was both intellectual and aristocratic. His father, Karl Bonhoeffer, was the leading empirical psychiatrist in Germany; he was a professor of psychiatry and neurology at Berlin University. As was often the case in such families, Dietrich Bonhoeffer learned to love music and languages from those within his family.

Bonhoeffer completed his doctorate at Berlin University in 1927; his thesis was titled *Communion of Saints: A Dogmatic Inquiry into the Sociology of the Church.* This work brought his understanding of the Christian faith into conversation with sociology. From the beginning of his intellectual life with the faith, Bonhoeffer connected the faith to real-life questions. He united philosophy and ideas with everyday experience. Bonhoeffer's work consistently takes clarity of conviction and finds ways to temper fervor with an ongoing recognition of the importance of change.

Bonhoeffer was ordained as a Lutheran minister by the Confessing Church in Germany in 1931. He served two Lutheran congregations in London from 1933 to 1935. Additionally, he visited Union Theological Seminary at the behest of one of the premier theologians in the United States, Reinhold Niebuhr. Bonhoeffer's fateful return to Germany in 1939 led to personal tragedy, but also to the writing that took his faith into the heart of everyday life.

He served as a pastor, was the head of a Confessing Church Seminary in Finkenwalde, and witnessed the closing of the Confession Church and its five seminaries by the Nazis in 1937. To gain a sense of Bonhoeffer's understanding of the seminary and his pastoral style, the work *Life Together* (1954) is a practical guide to how his philosophy and theology was brought into the life of everyday people.

Bonhoeffer became convinced that Hitler was an evil man capable of transforming the face of the West with an inhumanity previously unknown. His protests against Hitler and the Nazi regime ended in his death by hanging at the hands of the Nazis on April 9, 1945. This date, so close to the end of World War II, announces the degree of

Nazi anger toward Bonhoeffer and his fellow compatriots. Less than one month later, on May 2, the world learned of Germany's unconditional surrender, which closely followed the events of April 27, the date Hitler took his own life. The anger toward Bonhoeffer was kindled by his many acts of contention against the Third Reich, but, most centrally, his death came from his participation in the July 20, 1944, assassination attempt on Hitler. Bonhoeffer fought the Nazis out of conviction and hope for a Germany and a faith that offered pastoral care, not tyranny and death. This conviction and hope appeared early in his work through the church, especially the Barmen Declaration of 1934 that began the Confessing Church and openly stated opposition to National Socialism.

Bonhoeffer was formally recruited into the resistance in 1940 in an effort to assassinate Adolf Hitler and stop the Third Reich. The members of the conspiracy included Admiral Wilhelm Canaris, head of military intelligence; General Hans Oster (who recruited Bonhoeffer); and Hans von Dohnanyi (married to Bonhoeffer's sister, Christine); each was executed on April 9, 1945. On April 23 the Nazis executed Bonhoeffer's brother, Klaus, and a second brother-in-law, Rudiger Schleicher.

While in prison Bonhoeffer penned partial manuscripts, a novel, his ethics, and his recorded letters, which later became known as *Letters and Papers from Prison* (1953). Bonhoeffer's actions against the Third Reich and his participation in the assassination attempt against Hitler still leaves a jarring impression, for his commitment to ethics and the church guided an earlier book, *The Cost of Discipleship* (1959), considered by some to be the purest book on pacifism written in the twentieth century. Such a seeming contradiction makes his life and his work of continuing interest to many. Additionally, the contrast between writing and action displays Bonhoeffer's ongoing use of the dialectic in working through complex human problems. The "contradictions" in Bonhoeffer are more accurately understood as outcomes consistent with his dialectical work, both in the practical and the philosophical life of the faith. Bonhoeffer opens the door to questions of communication ethics with a deliberate engagement of the dialectic; his communicative life lives within the dance of difference. Bonhoeffer never seems to lose the practical importance of acknowledging this as God's world—both what we want, and that which we would not want to contend with, unite in the engaging of everyday communicative life.

What: The Ideas

Bonhoeffer's ideas, the "what" that drives his contribution to communication and communication ethics, begins with a particular form of engagement: the *dialectic*. Bonhoeffer understood the dialectic in a manner much akin to that of the Jewish theologian philosopher Martin Buber, as the "unity of contraries." Bonhoeffer seemed to understand why the A-frame house was used with such regularity when resources were limited. Such a structure requires that one side of the roof hold up the other. Bonhoeffer tempers conviction with doubt and uses conviction to temper doubt. This dialectic at work in his project yields insight without blind arrogance.

A basic set of Bonhoeffer's ideas include the "cost of discipleship," a "world come of age," "community," and "confession"; each of these terms is best understood through his commitment to the dialectic. The cost of discipleship begins his manner of understanding communicative life within a given faith narrative. He stressed the difference between "costly" and "cheap" grace. The former assumes that the grace of the faith is its guiding story and, at times, that the story will place one in harm's way, as it did in his own case. Cheap grace, on the other hand, assumes that the faith should somehow keep one from any sense of danger or threat. Bonhoeffer disapproved of any theology that employed *deus ex machina,* a "God in the machine" that comes to our rescue whenever there is a hint of difficulty. Bonhoeffer stressed a beginning assumption of discipleship which assumed that any narrative taken seriously comes with a cost—the grace is the story of the narrative, and with that grace comes the burden of discipleship.

Costly grace prepares one for a "world come of age," a world in which responsibility rests with the communicative agent, not with magic from the outside that takes all of one's responsibility away. A world come of age is a foreshadowing of what we now call postmodernity. It is an acknowledged place of difference that one must meet in the union of conviction and doubt. In a world come of age, one finds a narrative ground from which to communicate with others with full knowledge that difference must test and temper one's conviction. Bonhoeffer points to a world of learning as more fundamental than one of blind devotion. A world come of age is a place hospitable to difference, learning, and ongoing revelation.

Bonhoeffer understood revelation to be the ongoing creative impulse of community. Despite being termed the "community theologian of the twentieth century," in Bonhoeffer's view of community, at times God calls us to build community and, at other times, to burst it asunder. His love of community would not permit him to forget the importance of dialectical wisdom, a land of light and dark working hand in hand. Additionally, his commitment to community required tempering, lest he make community into an idol.

The tempering of what one considers the "good" was central to Bonhoeffer's view of confession. One needs to confess one's position to another and at the same time not fall in love with the act of confession itself. No matter what the idea, Bonhoeffer could find a way of texturing it with a dialectical imagination.

The cost of discipleship tied to costly grace shapes Bonhoeffer's communicative contribution—lived out in a changing world come of age, engaged not alone, but in community, and confessed without pride over the act of confessing. One way of uniting his contribution through the field of communication involves the term "dialectic confession."

Why: The Ongoing Significance of Bonhoeffer's Project

The significance of Bonhoeffer to this historical moment is that he answers an important question: How can a person of conviction (committed to a given narrative) meet a "world come of age" of increasing diversity without falling prey to loss of conviction or tumbling into the abyss of undue self-confidence? The ongoing relevance of Bonhoeffer rests in the basic conviction that the answer to this question is central to the moment in which we live.

Postmodernity is a time of increasing contention over what is "good" and what, if any, virtues should guide us. Bonhoeffer would meet this moment with the same courage with which he met the demands of Nazi Germany. Sometimes life simply calls for recognition of the pragmatic necessity of costly grace. The narrative of "good" guides, but it is not a suit of armor that protects one from all evil and misfortune. Additionally, one must be willing to learn about whatever one meets—the good, the bad, or the simply unexpected. For Bonhoeffer, this is God's world; we live within a place that calls for guided courage, admission of difference, the joy and limits of community, and the necessity to begin with confession, even the confession that one cannot applaud one's own confession.

Dialogue begins with meeting what is before us—whether we like it or not. Confession begins with admission of one's narrative ground and its limits. Dialogic confession assumes the meeting of what is before us with admission of bias, a willingness to learn, and a grittiness grounded in grace.

■ ■ ■

Arnett, Ronald C. 2005. *Dialogic Confession: Bonhoeffer's Rhetoric of Responsibility.* Carbondale: Southern Illinois University Press.

Bonhoeffer, Dietrich. 1953. *Letters and Papers from Prison.* Translated by Christian Kaiser Verlag. New York: Touchstone.

———. 1954. *Life Together.* Translated by John W. Doberstein. New York: Harper and Row.

———. 1959. *The Cost of Discipleship.* Translated by R. H. Fuller. New York: Simon and Schuster.

———. 1963. *Communion of Saints: A Dogmatic Inquiry into the Sociology of the Church.* Translated by R. Gregor Smith. New York: Harper and Row.

16

Paulo Freire
Face Saving and Communication

RONALD C. ARNETT

Paulo Freire was a champion of education for the masses and for individual persons. His commitment to education and literacy began with a basic assumption—the political futures of people rise and fall with their ability to engage in the public arena, which is made possible through literacy. The implications of Freire's project, begun in Brazil, continue to have profound implications for education internationally. In the United States, college and university rankings place increasing pressure upon student entrance scores. Freire points in a contrary direction that is more demanding of the faculty and the administration than of the students. The key is how much the students learn, not what they already know. Freire's question of a typical college or university would be, "Do you build the school off the backs of the administration and the faculty or off the backs of the students?" The demand for a student to be "already" good rather than to become a learning partner was unacceptable to Freire. Freire offers a prophetic voice of communication education that demands the privileged to take responsibility to assist all.

To outline Freire's contribution to communication, the following sections introduce a brief biography of him, illuminate the major concepts of his project, and indicate his ongoing importance for the study and practice of human communication. In this era of continuous political dispute, literacy takes on pragmatic importance as a baseline for fuller communicative participation in the public arena. Literacy is the communicative necessity for discernment and potential shaping of a society's political direction. Freire sought to change the reality of the disenfranchised, assisting them through literacy and political participation. In an era defined by disagreement, it is ongoing communicative engagement in the public arena that shapes political direction.

Paulo Freire was born in 1921 in Brazil. He died seventy-five years later in 1997, the same year of the copyright of his final book, *Pedagogy of Hope* (1998). The 1930s were particularly important in his development as he witnessed the devastating worldwide impact of the Great Depression. The 1940s brought Freire stature through education and marriage. He completed his law degree at the University of Recife and married his lifelong companion, Elza Maia Costa de Oliveira, with whom he had five children. Upon graduation from law school, Freire chose to teach Portuguese in secondary schools, and his wife worked as an elementary teacher. From the beginning of his career, literacy took center stage. The first major appointment of his career came in 1946; he became the director of the Department of Education and Culture of the Social Service in the Brazilian state of Pernambuco. His task of literacy came with pragmatic necessity—in Brazil, one had to prove literacy in order to be eligible for voting. The public arena had a governmentally imposed limit on participation determined by education and literacy. To place this demand in perspective, in the United States, literacy tests were used to exclude many citizens from voting until the Voting Rights Act of 1964, which attacked numerous forms of disenfranchisement. Freire understood that education was not just about learning, but that it more comprehensively defined the very nature of one's participation in a society. Whether officially tied to literacy tests or not, exclusion from the public arena stems from an inability to articulate political positions contending for power and guiding force within a society.

In 1962, as the director of culture at the University of Recife, Freire worked with three hundred sugarcane workers, teaching literacy in forty-five days! This was the first time he was able to put his ideas into effect. Then, in 1964, the reform-minded regime in Brazil was toppled by a coup. Freire was initially imprisoned and then made his way into exile in Chile, where he published his first book, *Education as the Practice of Freedom* (1973). There he worked in adult education, assisting Chile in becoming one of the top five countries in overcoming illiteracy. Freire equated the potential for liberation with literacy, education, and political participation in the public sphere.

Freire finished his best-known book, *Pedagogy of the Oppressed* (1974), as a visiting fellow at Harvard's Center for Studies in Education and Development. Later he worked for the World Council of Churches, continuing his work with literacy and education. He then returned to Brazil, accepting an appointment at the University of Sao Paulo. He published twenty-five books, and his career earned many honors, including the UNESCO Peace Prize in 1987 and the Christian Educators Award in 1985; the Paulo Freire Institute was named in his honor at UCLA.

Freire was an astute teacher of reading. He did not begin by equating reading with the joining of a dominant culture. In Freire's hands, the motivation to educate was pragmatic. Out of this practical effort came the possibility of change in the culture and in the ongoing lives of the people. His literacy project had Marxist roots, beginning with a prevailing historical consciousness that he contended could be met and changed by another form of literacy—the power of the word, in writing, in speech, and in deliberative change.

Freire was the educator who took reading to the streets, the farm, the house, any place and anywhere a person could engage with written works. He began not with abstract thought or "great" books, but with the learners' lives. Whatever people did for their daily living, he helped them learn how to read and understand the messages on the tools and items before them.

Freire offered an invitation to any seeking literacy and began the education with humble phrases and sentences. His hope was, however, far from small—his hope was to attack poverty and oppression through the power of literacy. This story of liberation initiated his campaign to assist others to read. With literacy, the book becomes a portable revolution—not an introduction into a privileged culture, but an opportunity to shape a culture that is not yet born, a culture that is ready for creation in the eyes of new readers armed with the power that shakes the foundations of the powerful.

The literacy project of Freire begins with a basic assumption—it is important to reflect and deliberate on the reading content. In teaching it is not enough to be content-rich; students need tools to question and analyze the legitimacy of a given work's contents. Literacy permits the student, the citizen, the member of the community to ask questions about content that shapes the public arena. Power rests in knowing the content and in knowing its origins and applications. Literacy, for Freire, begins with the ability to understand, affirm, or challenge the content that another offers. Literacy frees one from dependence on those in one's community (interpersonal power) or those in charge (resource power); change rests in the ability to call into question both the ideas of those close and the ideas of those far away who offer proclamations of content with the assumption that the ideas will go unexamined.

The central theme for Freire starts with his rejection of a "banking concept" of education. The banking concept was understood by Freire as a repository of unexamined and unquestioned content. The student or learner memorizes content, taking little, if any, time for reflection upon the material. Such content imposed upon the learner comes with the implicit and, in some cases, explicit demand to follow without question. Literacy provides the opportunity for another to question and to decide whether a given content and direction are worthy of a commitment and public affirmation. Freire understood the reason oppressive regimes worked so diligently to counter intellectual life: literacy opens the door to questioning, decreasing the possibility of blind allegiance.

Freire worked with a keen sense of hope that literacy could change the world of poverty and oppression. He sought to stop what he termed "narrative sickness." The term narrative, in this case, is a story that has no entrance for questioning. The sickness rests not with the fact that there is a narrative, but with the inability of another to question the content and the implications of a given content or narrative, to move a narrative into the realm of ideological dictate. Literacy works deconstructively as a counter to unreflective acceptance of a given story. The banking concept and narrative sickness work hand-in-hand to offer direction without democratic participation.

Narrative sickness is counteracted by a communicative act of "critical consciousness" that does not accept given content uncritically, without deliberation and reflection. Literacy permits one to discern the origins of ideas and their implications for one's self or one's community. The historical position of a given people requires interpretation and engagement; there is no singular sense of a "given" view of the world. A critical consciousness permits one to question, and literacy provides the necessary tools to do in-depth analysis and to communicate with others about one's position and/or to question the position of another. Critical consciousness permits one to ask questions about the validity and applicability of a given idea, making literacy a tool of cultural change.

Freire applied literacy to a campaign against communicative actions that he termed the banking concept and narrative sickness, which act to suppress critical consciousness. He wanted people to live in a land where a "culture of silence" could not prosper simply because people did not possess the tools for questioning those who shaped the content communicated to them. He took literacy into a revolutionary fight against a culture of silence.

Freire himself had experienced the power of silence in the hands of oppressors. One cannot ever assure that such a negative form of leadership will not arise despite literacy. For literacy does not come with a guaranteed outcome. However, with literacy in place, governments are not protected by a "culture of silence" when they take public and visible strides against a people. Lack of literacy permits oppression; without literate questioning, oppression goes unseen. Literacy moves oppression from the shadows into public discourse and fosters hope of change.

The power of Freire's literacy project rests in his hope of liberation through education. For communicators, the significance of his work lies within a particular understanding of dialogue connected to learning. Freire did everything he could to bring literacy to the "other." He sought to "save face" of the other, in order to assure an environment of learning (Arnett 2002). Saving face, however, does not assume the status of a technique in Freire's project. He only worked to save the face of the learner. A person who oppresses or disrupts learning does not have such a privileged status. Freire ignored or fought against those who got in the way of the literacy of others.

Freire's limits on saving face underscore the limits he put on dialogue. He stated that dialogue between oppressor and oppressed is not possible. The only way dialogue is possible in such a setting is to alter the relationship so that there is no oppressor, and no oppressed. Dialogue, for Freire, requires a literacy that puts the two sides on more equal footing and, even then, is not possible if oppression continues to guide the relationship.

Freire offered hope to the oppressed, but in a way that carried forth a call for responsibility. Literacy is the bane of authority that seeks a culture of unreflective helplessness. The hope of the oppressor is that the adage of hear no, see no, and do no evil permits the evil to come from the oppressor alone. Literacy first permits one to see (to read) and then to act with responsibility, for ideas are not neutral—they call us to acts of change. For Freire, literacy mattered, because all human beings deserve the right and the responsibility to shape the world about them.

■ ■ ■

Arnett, Ronald C. 2002. "Paulo Freire's Revolutionary Pedagogy: From a Story-Centered to a Narrative-Centered Communication Ethics." *Qualitative Inquiry* 8, no. 4: 489–510.

Freire, Paulo. 1973. *Education as the Practice of Freedom in Education for Critical Consciousness.* New York: Continuum.

———. 1974. *Pedagogy of the Oppressed.* Translated by Myra Bergman Ramos. New York: Seabury Press.

———. 1998. *Pedagogy of Hope: Reliving Pedagogy of the Oppressed.* New York: Continuum.

17

Hannah Arendt
Public as Authority

MAURINE BEASLEY

Hannah Arendt (1906–1975) was one of the most brilliant and controversial philosophers of her day. Her own life, influenced by two World Wars and the horrors of the Holocaust, represented a stage for her reflections on the nature of good and evil. As a teacher, writer, and journalist, she examined the human condition against a backdrop of political ideology, opposing both the concepts of totalitarian government and unlimited human responsibility. While she believed in the importance of individual morality, she also argued that no human being possesses the power to control the consequences of his or her own actions. Her influential work embraced a wide range of twentieth-century concerns, including the issues of mass society and political image-making.

The only child of a middle-class Jewish couple, Paul and Martha Cohn Arendt, she was born in Hannover, Germany, but grew up in Königsberg in East Prussia where her father, an engineer, died of syphilitic insanity when Hannah was only seven years old. Her mother, a forward-looking Social Democrat, encouraged her daughter's intellectual interests and was proud of the fact that she could read before she started kindergarten. A shy young woman, Arendt spent long periods alone reading and writing poetry. To gain admission to a university, she studied for two years with a private tutor and audited classes at the University of Berlin to prepare for the *abitur,* a difficult entrance examination.

Enrolled in 1924 at the University of Marburg, she studied theology and fell in love with Martin Heidegger, a distinguished philosopher. His popular lectures eventually became famous as the foundation of a school of thought known as *Existenzphilosophie* that called upon individuals to pay attention to their own existence and be responsible for their own destinies. Although their love affair was brief, she and Heidegger remained close friends and his work influenced her own. In 1929 Arendt married Gunther Stern, a writer. That same year, when she was only twenty-two, she received a doctorate in philosophy from the University of Heidelberg where she studied under Karl Jaspers, a psychiatrist who served as a second father to her. Her dissertation was titled *The Concept of Love in St. Augustine,* but her interest soon shifted to the field of German-Jewish history in the midst of the mounting wave of German anti-Semitism. She began a book, *Rachel Varnhagen: The Life of a Jewess,* a biography of an eighteenth-century salon hostess who fought against her Jewish heritage before returning to it. The work was not published until 1957.

After Hitler assumed power in 1933, Arendt was imprisoned for a week for pro-Zionist activities. After her release she and Stern escaped to Paris where she worked for Jewish organizations. The marriage ended in 1936 when she met Heinrich Blücher, a non-Jew from Berlin who was a Communist until 1939. Following their marriage in 1940, Arendt and Blücher were held in separate internment camps in France but managed to escape the German invasion of that country. Accompanied by her mother, they arrived in New York in 1941. During World War II Arendt wrote extensively on Jewish history and was helped by other expatriates like Paul Tillich, an eminent theologian, to place articles in publications such as *Jewish Social Studies* and *Jewish Frontier.* As she and Blücher mastered English, they made friends with American intellectuals including Alfred Kazin and Mary McCarthy.

From 1944 to 1946 Arendt was director of research at the Conference on Jewish Relations and taught history part-time at Brooklyn College. Subsequently she was a senior editor at Schocken Books. She continued to write for various intellectual magazines, including the *Partisan Review* and *The Nation,* and advocated an Arab-Jewish state in Palestine. Her first major work, *The Origins of Totalitarianism,* an outgrowth of her essays, appeared in 1951 and received immediate acclaim, tracing the relationship of anti-Semitism, imperialism, and totalitarianism. In it she argued that mass society with its breakdown of collective interests provided a hospitable environment for totalitarian government. In 1951 she also became an American citizen. The success of her book led to opportunities for her to lecture at Princeton and other leading universities.

In 1958 she published *The Human Condition,* perhaps her most important book, in which she discussed the nature of political freedom. Based on an impressive reconstruction of life and politics in ancient Greece, the book dealt with the life of activity, which Arendt called the *Vita Activa.* This she defined as labor, work, and action involved in producing political experience. She saw labor as a necessity for renewal of life, but not as high an order as work, which she contended shaped a common world for the formation of political communities. At the top of her hierarchy stood action, which she equated with the freedom to take political initiatives in a public setting so one's actions are apparent to others. Arendt theorized that citizens were free to perform in the public world of the city because others took care of their personal needs in the private sphere. The work envisioned good government as pluralistic, reached by free individuals joining together to choose and empower their own leaders. Arendt took a pessimistic view of modern life, contending that modern individuals were so wedded to work for economic gain and meaningless consumption that they had little opportunity to take part in genuine political debate.

In 1961 Arendt went to Jerusalem as a correspondent for the *New Yorker* to cover the trial of Adolf Eichmann, the German charged with planning and overseeing the killing of millions in Nazi death camps during World War II. Her controversial account of the trial, which was published first in the *New Yorker* in 1963 and then in book form under the title, *Eichmann in Jerusalem: A Report on the Banality of Evil,* met intense criticism from many Jews and others. They attacked her premise that Eichmann was not inherently a monster but simply a thoughtless person. To her, Eichmann was a bureaucrat concerned with logistical issues, emotionally and intellectually unequipped to perceive the horrors inflicted as a result of his routine decisions. Using her most famous phrase, "the banality of evil," Arendt argued that all human beings are capable of evil acts similar to those of Eichmann. She pointed out that Jewish leaders themselves often cooperated with Nazis in sending their own people to death camps. In later writings she attempted to clarify her position, publishing a group of essays in 1978 titled *The Jew as Pariah: Jewish Identity and Politics in the Modern Age.*

Other works included *On Revolution,* which appeared in 1963. It praised the 1956 Hungarian revolution against Russian rule as an example of people acting together to counter totalitarian rule. A short 1970 book, *On Violence,* contended that violence is self-defeating.

In the last phase of her life, however, Arendt immersed herself more fully in analysis of activities of the mind. She planned a three-volume exploration of human thought itself, aimed at exploring the meaning of human responsibility and judgment in an era in which traditional moral standards had broken down.

Arendt died in 1975 after a heart attack, having completed the first, and half of the second, of her three volumes. They were published in 1978 as *The Life of the Mind*. Books of letters also were published posthumously: *Between Friends: The Correspondence of Hannah Arendt and Mary McCarthy, 1949–1975* (1995) and *Hannah Arendt, Karl Jaspers: Correspondence, 1926–1969* (1992). In addition, lectures, addresses, and articles were collected in a 2003 book titled *Responsibility and Judgment.*

One of Arendt's most important theories dealt with the idea of freedom as a public activity, which gave her work particular significance for the field of mass communication. As a journalist herself, Arendt expressed both her own belief in and doubt about public discourse. *On Revolution* contended that the spirit of the American Revolution, which she considered a success in overthrowing tyranny, unfortunately had not been preserved, since over the years ordinary citizens had come to play little part in the political process beyond voting. To recover the idea of citizenship as it was known in antiquity, she called for participatory democracy. This eventually may make her work particularly appealing to a digital age linked by the Internet—a prospect that she could not have foreseen.

To Arendt the political forms of the twentieth century—whether devoted to social welfare, national identity, or totalitarian concepts—represented corruptions of the original idea of democracy that stressed the importance of individual speech in public space. In her view social matters involving mundane aspects of living should be left in the domestic or private realm separate from the exercise of full citizenship. In this respect her work has been criticized by feminists who argue that the personal side of human relationships should be equated with politics. In terms of mass communications there is no reason to suppose that Arendt found the blandness of corporate electronic or print journalism, with its focus on consumer values, a viable means of engaging an active citizenry in political life. Still, by her own participation in journalism, she valued the role of the mass media, as represented by high-quality journals, in stimulating thoughtful discussion of abstract political ideas.

Obviously Arendt's philosophical arguments drew on the events of the day as reflected in the mass media. She believed in the power of publicity, contending that action itself is meaningless unless others are able to bear witness and so give it meaning. Yet, she stood outside the conventional definition of being either a liberal or a conservative. In looking at the Civil Rights movement, for instance, she opposed the U.S. Supreme Court decision in 1954 that outlawed racial segregation in schools. While Arendt was against legislation based on race, particularly antimiscegenation laws, she criticized the school desegregation ruling on grounds it violated the private right of parents to oversee their children's education in a setting they found suitable.

In an essay titled "Reflections on Little Rock," published in *Dissent* magazine in 1959, she took as her starting point a widely distributed newspaper photograph of an unhappy African American girl walking home from a newly integrated school while being taunted by an unruly mob of white segregationists. Arendt declared that if she were the child's mother, she would never let the girl be humiliated by placement in a school where she obviously was not wanted. As an alternative to forced desegregation, she suggested a voluntary effort to build new schools for black and white pupils whose parents wanted them in integrated classes. She pointed out that if the Supreme Court had declared miscegenation laws unconstitutional, it hardly would have proceeded to insist on mixed marriages.

In a 1975 lecture, "Home to Roost," printed in *Responsibility and Judgment,* Arendt lauded both the *New York Times* and *Washington Post* for publication of the Pentagon Papers in 1971 that traced the history of U.S. involvement in Vietnam. She said they showed that the United States had attempted to gloss over defeat in a phony image-making attempt to convince the world of American superiority. She credited journalists with exposing governmental lying and performing a public service by printing the exposé. Similarly she valued the role played by the news media in exposing the political scandal of Watergate (the name given a Washington burglary, ultimately traced to the White House, which led to the resignation of President Richard M. Nixon in 1974 under threat of impeachment).

It is hard to make a case for Arendt as a mass communication scholar. She was not. Much of her work falls into the classical Western tradition of political thought and certainly is broader and more abstract than that of any single communication theorist. Yet, in her appreciation for the role of the journalist as a truth-teller and watchdog of power, she came close to assigning journalism a leadership role in attempting to correct what she saw as the multitudinous shortcomings of the modern era. Arendt can be seen as a strong defender of the First Amendment, which guarantees free expression.

For Arendt the nations of the twentieth century had handed public affairs over to bureaucrats and professional politicians who were expert in manipulation of public opinion. One can infer from her writings that she found investigative journalism one of the few tools left to counter governmental power, even though it was an unwieldy and not very effective one. Perhaps if she had witnessed the phenomenal outpouring of opinion on the Internet today, she would have rejoiced in its latitude for all shades of public expression. Then again perhaps she would have been repulsed by its potential for misuse and manipulation by the unscrupulous. Arendt's enthusiasm for Socrates and other figures from ancient history lay in their personification of extraordinary leadership. Unhappily, she saw little evidence of this in the modern world.

■ ■ ■

Arendt, Hannah. 1958. *The Human Condition.* Chicago: University of Chicago Press.

———. 1968. *Eichmann in Jerusalem: A Report on the Banality of Evil.* Rev. ed. New York: Viking. Original work published in 1963.

———. 2003. *Responsibility and Judgment.* Edited by Jerome Kohn. New York: Schocken.

———. 2004. *The Origins of Totalitarianism.* Rev. ed. New York: Schocken. Original work published in 1954.

The Legalist Stance
Loyalty to Authority

The legalist approach to ethics places the emphasis on following rules. This is the stance of normative ethics, of honoring an authority or a revered code of principles of some kind.

Moses brought the Ten Commandments to the Israelites from Yahweh. For Muhammad, the natural law created by Allah gives people an ethical system by which to act. Plato's highly structured society is built on proscriptions, and Kant devised a legalistic ethics by his categorical imperative to which we owe our unfailing duty. Hobbes believed that the ruler needed absolute power for society to be possible, and therefore his ethics is rules by which we can be obedient to the sovereign.

PART IV

Plato
Elite Norms

LEE ANNE PECK

One cannot discuss Greek philosopher Plato (428/7–348/7 BCE) and his writings without mentioning his mentor Socrates (469–399 BCE). Plato was born into one of the most distinguished aristocratic families in Athens—a family with whom the teacher-philosopher Socrates was supposedly friendly. As a youth, Plato and other young, bright Athenians became familiar with Socrates' method of questioning, a method involving face-to-face dialogue. Socrates used this technique to discover the truth and to expose ignorance. These young aristocrats learned and used this "Socratic Method," usually with those in authority. Some Athenian leaders, however, thought this cross-examination type of questioning was reckless and irresponsible. Eventually these disgruntled legislators charged Socrates with corrupting the youth of Athens and introducing false gods; Socrates was convicted and sentenced to death.

Socrates always believed, though, that he could best help the citizens of Athens by encouraging them to examine their lives through questioning and dialogue. He is quoted by Plato as saying, "The unexamined life is not worth living" (Grube 1981, Apology 38A). Socrates tried to convince citizens that each of them was accountable for his or her own moral actions; he believed unethical behavior came from ignorance, so he fought against this. For Socrates—and for Plato—knowledge, or the truth, was always contrasted with one's beliefs.

During Socrates' time, a roving group of teachers called Sophists taught the rhetorical technique of persuasion to students who paid for the privilege. Socrates is sometimes linked to them; however, he was different because, unlike the oftentimes unprincipled Sophists, he did not care if he won an argument and allegedly did not accept payment; he was only seeking the truth. He actually rejected the notion that he taught anything. Socrates also did not record his ideas in writing; he believed arguing in person was more valuable. Through his discussions, which always involved "What is 'X'?" people were supposed to discover the truth.

Socrates and the state of affairs surrounding his death had a great influence on Plato, so much so that Plato took on the task of writing Socrates' thoughts into more than two dozen dialogues of different lengths with Socrates as the main character. It is believed that Plato's earliest dialogues reflect Socrates' views the most accurately. As Plato continued to write over the years, he apparently began to insert his ideas into the dialogues although the self-assured Socrates remained the main character. It should be noted that others, such as the historian Xenophon (430–350 BCE) and the comic poet Aristophanes (448–380 BCE), also wrote about Socrates, but Plato's earlier dialogues are the most well known and most accurate, according to some scholars.

After the death of Socrates, Plato began to doubt the political atmosphere in Athens, which had a so-called democracy where it seemed only the loudest—not the most thoughtful—voices were heard. At a younger age, Plato thought he might want a political or public career, but Socrates and his teachings motivated the disillusioned Plato to continue with philosophy. Plato left Athens for several years; his exact itinerary is unknown. But it is believed he spent time in Italy, visiting the Greek colony and school created by Pythagoras; those who lived and studied at the colony tried to live simply in harmony with nature. Plato supposedly also visited a rustic agricultural community in Egypt.

He was invited to the court of King Dionysius I of Syracuse in Sicily as an adviser; later he became political theory tutor to King Dionysius II, but for a variety of reasons, Plato left his position with the newest king. Many believe that Plato incorporated these travels and experiences into his famous *Republic* (written in 360 BCE), which describes his utopian state or community where philosophers were kings.

When Plato returned to Athens, he created what might be considered the first university, the Academy, a school where students studied philosophy, mathematics, and the sciences—along with Plato's dialogues and other writing, of course. The philosopher Aristotle was probably the most famous student at the academy; he studied there during the last twenty years of Plato's life.

It could be argued that justice is the basis for Plato's moral philosophy. However, the word "justice" in his time had a broader meaning than it does today. The three main virtues for Plato were moderation, courage, and wisdom—these combine to create the highest virtue of justice, or *dikaiosyne*. Therefore, *dikaiosyne* was also about morality and "the good life." The final "good," so to speak, is happiness.

To get to this final good, however, one must have knowledge of the forms, which is explained most thoroughly in Plato's "Phaedo," the dialogue in which the imprisoned Socrates drinks hemlock and dies. According to Plato, a person's soul, or mind, is the part of a person that understands the forms, and a person is born with this knowledge—it is eternal. Any objects of knowledge are forms, which are separate from the perceptible world. In other words, the forms never change, but in our everyday lives, things are temporary and changing and are grasped by our senses. For instance, if we consider a woman or flowers to be beautiful, they are beautiful through our understanding of what the universal form of beauty is. The form of beauty never changes while the woman's beauty may fade and the flowers may die.

Philosophy is the search for knowledge via the forms; therefore, knowledge is the essence of things, not the belief of what things are. Plato wrote through Socrates:

> The body keeps us busy in a thousand ways because of its need for nurture. . . . Only the body and its desires cause war, civil discord and battles, for all wars are due to the desire to acquire wealth, and it is the body and the care of it, to which we are enslaved, which compel us to acquire wealth, and all this makes us too busy to practice philosophy. . . . if we are to ever have pure knowledge, we must escape from the body and observe matters in themselves with the soul by itself. (Phaedo 66 c-d)[1]

In other words, we have the innate ability to reason if we would take the time.

---

1. This page number citation to Plato's work is from the Stephanus edition.

A discussion of the forms continues in Plato's *Republic*. Through this work we begin to understand that Plato did not have much faith in the majority to act morally. If given a chance, and if they could get away with it, he believed many would act immorally. Therefore, such tendencies warranted some kind of authority. Acting ethically came from reason, but reason would have to be enforced in Plato's utopian city of the *Republic*. In other words, the virtues must be based on a political order regulated by those with a sense of morality—the *Republic*'s philosopher king and the guardians. According to contemporary philosopher Stanley Rosen, Socrates seemed to acknowledge that philosophers before him tended to forget about themselves in the big picture of things, and in the *Republic* they get a chance to actually be in control.

To explain in more detail: The philosopher king and the guardians in the *Republic* are the only ones able to handle both political and moral issues. Plato envisioned a community ruled by philosophers. The *Republic* begins with a discussion of the virtue of justice: If everyone does his or her function, the city will be in harmony and will be a just society; people will live lives ruled by reason. Virtue is connected to the notion of something functioning well. For objects, virtue is good quality; for humans, virtue is a good state of character. The harmony of the soul is then compared to the harmony of the city, and if there is harmony in either, there is justice. Hence, justice is a blanket term for morality.

Although Platonism may not appeal to some because of its elitism as shown in the *Republic*, ethical communicators can find additional worthwhile writings from Plato, including a famous excerpt from the *Republic* to be discussed later in this chapter. In the early dialogue titled "Crito" (written in 360 BCE),[2] Plato via Socrates teaches principles that should be important to communication professionals: independence, social responsibility, and justification for one's actions. This is certainly a dialogue that shows Socrates' beliefs about what is moral. As Socrates sits in jail about to be executed for corrupting the youth of Athens, he defends these principles through a reasoned argument with his friend Crito, who has come to beg him to escape.

However, Socrates asks Crito to remember past conversations they have had about the importance of keeping one's principles. Therefore,

2. G. M. A. Grube, *Plato: Five Dialogues*.

should he, Socrates, change his principles because of his current situation? If he escaped prison with Crito and others' help, he would be defying Athenian law and the citizens of Athens. Even if he believed that the court of Athens made a mistake sentencing him to die, the decision made was a legal one. If he escaped and went to another city, could he honestly teach about virtue and discovering the truth? If he stayed and died in Athens, he believed he would actually improve the city's moral environment. Revenge is never acceptable. Socrates used reflective reasoning—and courage—to come to his justified conclusion; he could be considered morally innocent and certainly socially responsible.

Another dialogue, the "Gorgias" (written in 380 BCE),[3] is pertinent to the communication professional. Socrates defends justice via a discussion of rhetoric. At the dialogue's beginning, a discussion begins between Gorgias and Socrates about teachers of discourse. Gorgias believes if the rhetorician is teaching what morality is, then the rhetorician must be moral. One might then ask if a person who teaches about morality is really moral or just a moralizer. Socrates explains that a person well-trained in rhetoric may misuse his skills—as many Sophists did. For instance, one can teach students it is wrong to commit adultery but be committing adultery at the same time! Many other ways exist, however, to misuse one's rhetorical skills.

Socrates says it takes a certain aptitude to be a rhetorician. He compares it with other skills people have such as cooking. For instance, creating a good meal creates pleasure. Just as the object of the meal is not necessarily to make one healthy, rhetoric might only cater to a person's desire to be pleased in some way. Therefore a Sophist could be considered merely a crafty person with a knack for persuasion—not true knowledge. The character Callicles enters the discussion with Gorgias and Socrates; he believes doing philosophy is impractical in day-to-day living, and one's goal should be to have power and control. But Socrates disagrees and explains there is a difference between bad and good pleasures. For instance, it may be pleasurable to have power, but many rhetoricians can't tell if it is a virtuous power because they don't live examined lives. It is not enough to be brave or powerful; one must also seek the truth.

3. Plato, *Gorgias,* translated by R. Waterfield.

One of Plato's most famous excerpts from the *Republic* is the "Allegory of the Cave" from Book VII. In a deep cave, men have been chained by their legs and necks to a wall; they cannot move and can only look straight ahead. A fire burns behind these prisoners, and the light from the fire reflects above them on the wall; between the fire and the prisoners is a walkway bordered by a screen. Behind this screen, puppeteers walk, carrying high above them artificial objects. These items project above the screen on the prisoners' wall. For the prisoners, these shadows are their reality—or their beliefs.

For today's communicators, the cave is a community, the prisoners are members of the public, and the puppeteers are communication professionals doing what they're assigned to do. The daylight outside the cave is true knowledge. The shadows the public sees on the wall are what is provided to them. In Plato's allegory, a prisoner escapes from the cave and sees the world outside the cave. He becomes enlightened, and the shadows are no longer his reality. When he returns to the cave to explain what he saw to his peers, they are distrustful. Plato would say, however, that ethical communicators need to be like the prisoner who escapes, comes back to the cave, and shares the truth. Whether it's entertaining or pleasurable or not, this would be the socially responsible thing to do. A communication professional's job is to give citizens the information they need to function in society. In other words, media practitioners need to go beyond merely providing shadows; they need to act socially responsible and share the truth.

These are only a few examples from Plato's dialogues that may have direct relevance to today's communicators; to discuss all the written work of the prolific Plato goes beyond what can be done in one chapter. However, communication professionals can learn the importance of reflection and reasoning about their actions via Plato through Socrates. According to Plato, our essence is to live by reason; when we do this, we are virtuous and happy.

Although Plato does not provide a formula for determining how one should act in day-to-day dilemmas—for instance, the universal Form of the Good is of no help to people trying to wrestle with a specific ethical problem—communicators who embrace Plato's teachings would never misuse their power and would always seek the truth. Socrates, it certainly could be said (via Plato), was against self-indulgence but favored self-knowledge as a goal. For Plato, knowledge is necessary for the virtuous communicator.

■ ■ ■

Grube, G. M. A. 1981. *Plato: Five Dialogues.* Indianapolis: Hackett Publishing.

Irwin, T. 1977. *Plato's Moral Theory: The Early and Middle Dialogues.* Oxford, UK: Clarendon Press.

Plato. 1998. *Gorgias.* Translated by R. Waterfield. Oxford, UK: Oxford University Press.

———. 1993. *Republic.* Translated by R. Waterfield. Oxford, UK: Oxford University Press.

19

Muhammad
Honor-Centered Morality

MOHAMMAD A. SIDDIQI

"I've been sent for perfecting the good morals."

Muhammad, the son of Abdullah, was born in Makkah (now in Saudi Arabia) in 570 AD[1] to Aminah in the house of his grandfather Abdul Muttalib, the leader of the tribe of Quraish. His father Abdullah had passed away in Madinah six months before Muhammad's birth. His mother died when Muhammad was about six. Thereafter his grandfather took charge of him and later his uncle Abu Talib became his guardian. However, he spent much of his early childhood in the house of his wet nurse Haleema, to whom he was entrusted according to the Arab custom. Haleema lived in a desert village away from Makkah. The pristine and rugged desert environment contributed to his quick growth, sound health, and disciplined manners.

Muhammad was twelve or thirteen years old when his uncle, Abu Talib, started taking him on business trips to Syria (Sham) as well as to many nearby markets. During these trips, Muhammad not only proved to be an honest and smart trader but also learned about Byzantine and Christian history. He met with many monks and religious personalities, including the famous monk Bahirah at Busra (now in Iraq). Bahirah informed Muhammad that he was going to be a great reformer and prophet of God and told his uncle to take good care of him.[2] While at home in Makkah, Muhammad was a herdsman,

---

1. Muhammad Husayn Haykal, *The Life of Muhammad*, 48.
2. Safi-Ur-Rahman Al-Mubarakpuri, *Ar-Raheeq Al-Makhtoom* (*The Sealed Nectar*). *Biography of the Noble Prophet*, 60.

which provided him plenty of time to ponder and to contemplate.

From an early age people of Makkah called Muhammad the truthful (*Al-Sadiq*) and the trustworthy (*Al-Ameen*). They invited him to settle disputes and to provide guidance in solving their problems. Muhammad was fifteen when he saw his first war between two major Arab tribes. Later he played a very positive role in the treaty of Al-Fudoul that not only brought the war to an end but also produced a permanent charter for peaceful coexistence among various warring factions of Arabs.

At the age of twenty-five a wealthy Arab widow, Khadijah, hired Muhammad to lead her trade caravan to Syria. He returned from Syria with unprecedented profits. His good manners, honesty, sincerity, and acumen impressed Khadijah. She asked her uncle to take her marriage proposal to Muhammad's uncle. Khadijah was forty and Muhammad twenty-five when they got married. Khadijah bore all his children, four daughters and two sons, except Ibrahim. All of Muhammad's sons died quite young. Three of his daughters also died during his lifetime. Muhammad did not marry any other woman until the death of Khadijah twenty-five years later. He also avoided gambling, wine, and idol worshipping. At thirty-five, he intervened in a clash among tribal Arabs that occurred during the rebuilding of the holy house of God, the Ka'bah.

Muhammad spent most of his spare time contemplating and meditating at the top of a mountain overlooking Makkah in the cave of Hira. One day while he was in the cave, he heard a voice commanding him to read. Muhammad answered in surprise, "What shall I read?" He felt as if he was squeezed and then again ordered to read. Muhammad said, "I can not read." He was squeezed twice more and commanded to read. Then he heard the voice saying, *"Read in the name of your Lord, who has created (all that exists); has created human being from a clot (a piece of thick coagulated blood). Read and your Lord is most gracious."* This was the beginning of revelation and these verses are now part of chapter 96 of the Qur'an. Muhammad repeated these words after they were said to him. He was told that the messenger was the angel Gabriel. Thus began an overwhelming experience that Muhammad went through for the remaining twenty-three years of his life in which the entire Qur'an was revealed to him.

It was after this revelation that Muhammad proclaimed prophethood at the age of forty in 710 AD. Thereafter, he lived for thirteen more years in Makkah. His life in Makkah was full of struggle, pain, and suffering. The pagan leaders could not tolerate a direct threat to idol worshipping. Muhammad's message was simple: Worship one and only one God who has created you; I am His messenger; and you will return to God for an eternal life in the hereafter. After thirteen years God commanded Muhammad to migrate to Madinah, a city about 250 miles north of Makkah. In Madinah, Muhammad first established a brotherhood between the people who accompanied him from Makkah (the immigrants or the *Muha'jiroon*) and the Muslims of Madinah (the helpers or the *Ansa'rs*). This enabled Makkan immigrants to restart their lives afresh with the resources provided by their brethren in Madinah. Muhammad also signed treaties with the Christians, Jews, and pagans for a peaceful coexistence. These treaties established the rights and duties of each of the faith groups living in Madinah. The focus of the Qur'anic revelations in Madinah also shifted from ideological to civil matters including business transactions, family life and marriage, as well as fairness and justice-related issues.

The tribal leadership of Makkah and Arabia, as well as the established Persian and Roman empires, viewed Muhammad's increasing political power as a threat. Muhammad had to fight many wars in order to defend Islam, Muslims, and the newly established Islamic state. In the eighth year after the migration, Muhammad reentered Makkah victorious, removed all idols from the house of God, and declared a general amnesty to all including many of Islam's worst enemies. In the next few years, Muhammad dealt with other tribal populations in the Arabian Peninsula and most of them embraced Islam without any war. He sent more than a dozen ambassadors to regional powers and a few even to the superpowers of the time. Most of them either embraced Islam or agreed to Islamic rule while maintaining their separate religious identities.

The last major event in Muhammad's life was his farewell pilgrimage to Makkah. Accompanied by 90,000 to 114,000 Muslims, Muhammad performed his last pilgrimage (*Hajj*).[3] In his farewell speech Muhammad reiterated some of the major ideological principles of Islam and laid down the ethical framework. He declared that slavery had no place in Islam; forgiveness was one of the best virtues; God created all people equal and they should be treated as such; the book of God and the traditions of God's Prophet should

---

3. Haykal, *Life of Muhammad*, 483.

be the foundations of Islamic beliefs and practices; being just under all circumstances was the underlying ethical principle of Islam.[4] When Muhammad died at the age of sixty-three, many of his companions were utterly shocked—some even declared war against anyone who dared to say that Muhammad was dead. However, Abu Bakr, Muhammad's closest friend and soon to be declared the first caliph of Islam, came forward and recited the following verse from the Qur'an, calming the people and convincing them that Muhammad had left this world for ever:

> Muhammad is no more than a messenger and indeed many messengers have passed away before him. If he dies or is killed, will you turn away from your faith; and if you do so, you will not harm God. Indeed God will reward those who are grateful to Him. (Qur'an 3:144)

Muhammad's greatest gift to humanity may be considered as the Qur'an and his own life, which according to his wife Ayesha was "an embodiment of Qur'an." The Qur'an and the Sunnah (Muhammad's sayings and deeds) contain the broad principles needed to negotiate the problems that arise in human societies in different ages.[5] The Qur'an emphasizes the ethical dimensions of sending Muhammad by declaring, "And we have sent you (O, Muhammad) not but as a mercy to all creatures" (Qur'an 21:107). The Qur'an also states, "And the Word of your Lord has been fulfilled in truth and in justice" (Qur'an 6:115).

In the Qur'an, as Ansari points out, God and the Hereafter are not merely postulates of morality as Kant had thought; they determine the meaning and content of ethical concepts and values.[6] The famous tradition narrated by Muhammad's wife Ayesha is a strong testimonial that Islamic ethical traditions are first and foremost rooted in the Qur'an. When asked about the morals and manners of the Prophet, Ayesha replied, "His morals are nothing but Qur'an." Muhammad himself described the purpose of his prophethood by saying, "I have been sent for perfecting the good morals." In numerous verses, the Qur'an provides definitive status to the Prophet

---

4. Ibid., 487.
5. Marwan Ibrahim Al-Kayasi, *Morals and Manners in Islam.*
6. Abdul Haq Ansari, "Islamic Ethics."

Muhammad as the route through which one can attain God's Love and Mercy. For example, the Qur'an clearly says, "Say (O, Muhammad) if you really love God, then follow me" (3:31); "But no, by your Lord, they can have no faith until they make you (Muhammad) the judge in all disputes that they have" (4:65); "He who obeys the messenger (Muhammad) has indeed obeyed God" (4:80).

Among the other sources of Islamic ethical traditions are the lives and examples set by the companions of Muhammad, especially the first four caliphs: Abu Bakr, Omer, Othman, and Ali, also known as the rightly guided caliphs. They made sincere efforts to excel in the Islamic ethical traditions. As Ansari states, they "were trained by the Prophet himself, and their lives as individuals and as a society are the best embodiment of Islamic ethical traditions."[7] Lastly, the two sources of inspiration and directions to formulate Islamic ethics are those that are the basis of Islamic Shariah or the Islamic law. The first is Ijma or the consensus of the scholars on issues that have no direct mention in the Qur'an and the Sunnah. The second is Qiyas or analogical reasoning done by a process known as *ijtihad*, which means an effort made by a qualified scholar or body of scholars to formulate a guideline to deal with a new issue or situation. These sources of authority and inspiration provide a dynamic process for both the formulation as well as the preservation of Islamic ethical traditions in all the areas of ethical discourse: descriptive, normative, and meta-ethics.

The actions, sayings, and teachings of Muhammad show that Islam came to illuminate peoples' lives by elevating their conduct through the practical guidance that the life of the Prophet provided for them. God testifies to this in the Qur'an by saying, "Indeed! In the Messenger of God you have the best example to follow; for every person who hopes (for the meeting with) God, and the Last day and remembers God much" (Qur'an 33:2 1).

The life of Muhammad is the most perfect and vibrant aspect of the Islamic ethical traditions. Muhammad himself is the utmost embodiment of Islam's moral and ethical teachings. Numerous Hadith (sayings of Muhammad) further clarify his own emphasis on ethical and moral conduct. Here are a few of his sayings from the most authentic book of Hadith, Al-Bukhari.

7. Ibid., 82.

The best things given to people are excellent moral character.

A Muslim with the best moral character has the perfect faith.

On the Day of Judgment there will be nothing weightier in the balance of a Muslim than his/her goodness of character.

If you want to say something about your brother, say something good or keep quiet.

Verify news before believing in it or acting upon it.

Make people's lives easy; do not make it difficult.

Muhammad's life as a messenger of God, as a husband, as a spiritual, political, and military leader, as a head of state, and as an individual person is glorified by his excellent ethical traditions. It is surprising that in a short span of just twenty-three years Muhammad was successful in establishing not only the religion of Islam but also an Islamic state, which was headquartered in Madinah. In addition, he fulfilled the excellence of human conduct in every aspect of human activity. To this the Qur'an testifies in these words, "This day I have perfected your religion for you, completed my favors upon you and have chosen for you Islam as your religion" (Qur'an, 5:3). He literally acted upon every single verse of the Qur'an.

Muhammad was an excellent-mannered, humble, soft-spoken, and philanthropic person. Even though he was a Prophet and a leader, he was also the first to serve people. He was a commander in chief often found in the front rows of the battlefield. He helped carry weak people's loads. He was most forgiving even to his staunchest enemies, as evidenced by his conduct on the day he entered Makkah victorious. Humble and softhearted, he exchanged ideas with his companions, mixed with them freely, and listened to and acted upon their suggestions in many instances. He never took personal revenge against anyone, never spoke a lie, never accused anyone, never uttered an obscene or indecent word, and never humiliated a person in his life. Whenever possible he chose the easy way of doing things and tried to make life easier for others around him. He played with children, took his wives to watch game shows, and always had a smiling face. He never talked without necessity. Even though the world presented him with all its allurement and amusements, he was indifferent to extravaganzas and luxuries. Even when he died, he chose humble conditions and pledged his armor to a Jew.

Every aspect of Muhammad's life has been meticulously preserved by his companions, who memorized almost every word that he uttered and narrated every one of the Prophet's actions. Later the scholars of Hadith developed a detailed science of verifying the authenticity of each and every Hadith. Out of more than 100,000 Hadith, only about 8,000 were classified as most authentic.

On the basis of the most authentic Hadith and the Qur'an one can describe the salient features of Islamic ethics integrated into Muhammad's mission and work throughout his life as a prophet:[8]

1. Islamic ethics is universal, divine, and permanent.
2. Islamic ethics is comprehensive.
3. Islamic ethics is positive and practical.
4. Islamic ethical traditions are free of double standards.
5. Islamic ethical traditions are progressive and dynamic.

During the days of Muhammad, people did not learn ethics through books, but by observing the lives of the Prophet and his companions. However, when historians and Islamic scholars compiled Muhammad's life and sayings, they catalogued the ethical traditions in the books of Hadith and the biographies of the Muhammad and his companions. In the early literature of Islam, Muslim jurists and scholars did not discuss ethics separately; instead they discussed them under various subtitles such as the chapter on cleanliness, the chapter on family, the chapter on marriage, etc. In these chapters they discussed the standard of conduct as prescribed by the Qur'an and the Sunnah pertaining to these specific areas.

Muhammad emphasized that a strong belief both in one God and in the accountability before God in the hereafter provided a general framework for ethical conduct. Both the Qur'an and Muhammad's Sunnah offer definitive guidelines for formulating ethical principles in a given time and space. While the fundamentals will remain the same, the details will vary.

Communication during the time of the Prophet and in early Islamic societies was rooted in these doctrinal principles, and as noted by Mowlana, "The ecological terrain of communication in an Islamic

8. Muzammil Siddiqi, "Introduction," vii–x.

state emphasizes intrapersonal/interpersonal communication over impersonal communication, social communication over mass communication, and intercultural communication over nationalism and interstate communication."[9] Muhammad emphasized the propagation of truth and the common good for the people as a whole. He insisted on verification of information before spreading it among people. As such, he disliked rumors, and slanderous characterization of individuals or groups. His most famous saying is "Actions are based on intentions." He asked people to have open and sincere dialogue.

If one has to present a communication model based on the Sunnah of Muhammad, it would be an interactive, open, universal, mutually beneficial, and symmetrical model of communication. Also, it would emphasize a universal code of ethics to be followed by all communication actors. It would not allow the use of communication to support a particular nation or people. Rather, it would urge people to use communication for the benefit of all. It would probably use the following Qur'anic verse as a guiding principle to formulate all communication strategies: "Call unto the way of your Lord with wisdom and best exhortation and (even if you have to confront) confront with them in the best possible way" (Qur'an 16:125).

■   ■   ■

Al-Kayasi, Marwan Ibrahim. 1992. *Morals and Manners in Islam.* New Delhi: Qazi Publications.

Al-Mubarakpuri, Safi-Ur-Rahman. 1996. *Ar-Raheeq Al-Makhtoom (The Sealed Nectar). Biography of the Noble Prophet.* Riyadh, Saudi Arabia: Dar-us Salam Publications.

Ansari, Abdul Haq. 1989. "Islamic Ethics." *American Journal of Islamic Social Sciences* 6, no. 1: 81–92.

Haykal, Muhammad Husayn. 1976. *The Life of Muhammad.* Indianapolis: North American Trust Publication.

Mowlana, Hamid. 1989. "Communication, Ethics, and the Islamic Tradition." In Thomas W. Cooper, ed., with Clifford G. Christians, Frances Forde Plude and Robert A. White, *Communication Ethics and Global Change* (New York: Longman), 137–46.

Noble Qur'an. 2001. Translated by Taqiuddin Al-Hilali and Mohsin

9. Hamid Mowlana, "Communication, Ethics, and the Islamic Tradition," 138.

Khan. Madinah, Saudi Arabia: King Fahad Complex for Printing of the Holy Qur'an.

Siddiqi, Muzammil. 1997. "Introduction." In Aslam Abdullah, *Morals and Manners: An Islamic Perspective.* Adopted and compiled from Muhammad Al-Ghazali's Khuluq al Muslim. Plainfield, Indiana: ISNA.

Immanuel Kant
Importance of Duty

LEE ANNE PECK

The modern philosopher Immanuel Kant (1724–1804) was a deontologist (*deon* is the Greek word for duty) and is famous for his ethical theory the Categorical Imperative. This is a duty-based theory insisting that moral actions cannot be based on consequences. According to Kant, the Categorical Imperative is the supreme principle that everyone should follow in all areas of life. If everyone adheres to this principle, then citizens will live in a lawful and moral society where one and all have unconditional worth. To apply Kant's moral theory, however, one must understand Kant's studies in politics and have a proper "moral catechism"—not to be confused with a religious catechism.

Kant was born in Königsberg in East Prussia (now Kaliningrad, Russia), the son of a humble harness-maker and his wife, who were both Lutheran Pietists. A bright young man, Kant began his studies at the age of sixteen at the University of Königsberg where many of the professors were also Pietists. He began his academic career studying the classics, but soon changed his major, so to speak, to philosophy. He took a break from his studies when his father died in 1746 and made a living by tutoring. Eventually, at the age of thirty-one, Kant graduated from Königsberg; he became a professor at the university and taught there most of his life. As a new lecturer, he taught physics and geography. In fact, the first book he published was titled *The Universal History of Nature and Theory of the Heavens,* which described the universe via Newton. After teaching about the external world, however, Kant became more interested in the internal—especially the complexities of morality. *The Grounding for the Metaphysics of Morals,* his first important work concerning ethics, was published in 1785.

Kant lived as a bachelor, and it has been said he never traveled more than sixty miles from his hometown. He was so disciplined and regimented, people could set their clocks by his daily movements! It should be noted that Kant lived a good portion of his life (1740–1786) under the rule of the Frederick the Great, whom Kant believed to be somewhat enlightened. However, when Frederick William II came into power after his father's death, he was not as indulgent as his father when it came to freedom of expression or thought. Therefore, Kant's writings toward the end of his life were almost self-censored because he knew his work would be read for censorship of unfavorable views or ideas.

The intellectual Enlightenment movement had an influence on and was influenced by Kant; he followed its precepts of reason, tolerance, and freedom. He believed all human beings were created equal, and no one should be treated as a means to an end. Kant scholar Warner Wick summarized that Kant and his Categorical Imperative require that people act in a way in which everyone would agree; this would create a free and equal society. This is "freedom under self-imposed law," Wick wrote.[1] A perfect, or ideal, moral community has law as its main principle of order, and a law needs to be universally applied.

According to Kant, morality is separate from desires, and only a good will is moral, and a good will is determined by duty. In other words, one acts from duty, not from a desire to do or be good. Therefore, the first or supreme formula of the Categorical Imperative, or the Formula of Universal Law, states: "Act only on a maxim that you can at the same time will to become a universal law" (G421).[2] As moral agents, people should act on maxims that all rational people would act on. If one can't will that everyone acts on the maxim, then acting on that maxim is morally wrong and not permissible. As mentioned above, Kant believed that people are rational beings. In other words, people have the capacity to reason, and reasoning should prevail over desire.

1. Warner Wick, "Introduction."
2. All citations from *Grounding for the Metaphysics of Morals* are hereafter cited G with page number(s) from the Prussian Academy edition.

The Categorical Imperative is introduced in Kant's *Grounding for the Metaphysics of Morals* (1785), a slim book from which most people get their introduction to Kant's moral theory. In the *Grounding,* Kant presents additional formulations of the Categorical Imperative that need to be mentioned. Kant's second formula, the Formula of Humanity (sometimes called the Formula of the End in Itself), states: "Act so as to treat humanity in oneself and others only as an end in itself, and never merely as a means." Another formulation is the Formula of Legislation for a Moral Community (or Formula of the Kingdom of Ends): "Every rational being must act as if by his maxims he were at all times a legislative member of the universal kingdom of ends." The formulas are different aspects of the same moral law. Writes Kant:

> The aforementioned three ways of representing the principle of morality are at bottom only so many formulas of the very same law: one of them by itself contains a combination of the other two. Nevertheless there is a difference in them, which is subjectively rather than objectively practical. (G436)

In the *Grounding,* Kant explains that the Categorical Imperative "alone purports to be a practical law, while all the rest may be called principles of the will but not laws," or hypothetical imperatives (G428). A simple example of a hypothetical imperative could be the following: "You are not allowed to take anything from this room—unless you have permission from the dean." So, in other words, you are not allowed to take anything from the supply closet, but you can if you have permission to do so. This is a hypothetical imperative and does not involve ethical decision-making.

In the *Grounding,* Kant gave four specific examples of maxims that can be universalized: don't kill yourself; don't lie to get money, or rather, don't make false promises; cultivate your talents; and help others. These can be split into perfect and imperfect duties. A perfect or narrow duty (don't kill yourself, don't make false promises) is one that prohibits a specific action and should be followed in all circumstances. On the other hand, an imperfect, or wide, duty is not so specific—how you accomplish helping others and cultivating your talents is not prescribed exactly. Although suicide may not be on the minds of communication professionals, they should follow the other maxims: they should avoid false promises, help other when necessary, and become the best they can be in their chosen professions.

The misunderstanding of Kant's ethics by communicators comes in many forms, from thinking that if they apply the Categorical Imperative they are merely going through moral mechanics, to thinking Kant's ideas are too legal-like and not really about morality. According to Kantian scholar Marcia Baron, some people are turned off by his deontic terms (such as "ought," "right," "wrong," and "duty") and see the Categorical Imperative as "one big rule," which doesn't look at the specifics of a situation. However, for Kant, being virtuous requires reflection and reasoning.

Some communicators may become confused when two maxims—for instance, do not kill and do not lie—seem to contradict one another. For example, what if during World War II someone was hiding a Jewish man in his home from German soldiers whose intent was to capture and kill him? Is it permissible to lie to the Nazi soldiers, telling them no one is hiding in the house? If the truth is told, the man could die, and the person hiding the Jewish man would be an accomplice to murder. Confusing stuff! But if we consider that maxims show us what we *ought* to do, there is indeed some flexibility in such situations. In Kant's lecture notes on ethics, he actually wrote that if someone is going "to make a wrongful use of the truth," then it is permitted to lie to that person. Choose the stronger duty, in other words.

However, consider this: A moral amateur will not be able to evaluate a maxim properly. In G422 and G423, Kant gave examples of the application of the Categorical Imperative. First, a person must know that a proposed action raises moral questions; therefore, the person knows to test the acceptability of the action. This is a key point in using the Categorical Imperative—a communicator who wants to apply the Categorical Imperative must have the appropriate background.

If one studies beyond the *Grounding* and moves on to Kant's *Metaphysics of Morals* (1797), Kant explains the importance of casuistry, or applied ethics (MM410).[3] Kant believed in teaching the "uneducated" via the case method. Because of the "gray" areas in

3. All citations from *Metaphysics of Morals* are hereafter cited MM with page number(s) from the Prussian Academy edition.

ethical decision-making, communicators may find themselves questioning how a maxim should be applied to a particular case. In this situation, communicators could create a new maxim, and as long as the maxim could be universalized in their profession, it would be a maxim to uphold. If the maxim could not be universalized, then it is not a maxim to keep.

It might be easier to consider this situation in the workplace. If all professionals needed to make a similar decision about something to do with their job performances, they would all agree with the maxim created for that performance. For instance, "Never lie in a press release" is a maxim to keep. However, one cannot always make decisions via what has been done in the past, according to Kant, and having empirical knowledge of human behavior does not help either. Communicators could find themselves in situations they have never experienced (MM215–16).

As Baron noted, the virtuous person is influenced by a conception of duty; he or she is committed to acting morally, and the Categorical Imperative requires thinking. Would a person want everyone to do this action? Therefore, if there is any deliberation happening, it's the principle being tested for universalizability, not the particular action itself. Kant wrote:

> For unless the dignity of virtue is exalted above everything else in actions, then the concept of duty itself vanishes and dissolves into mere pragmatic precepts [because] man's consciousness of his own nobility then disappears and he is for sale and can be bought for a price that the seductive inclinations offer him. (MM482)

In the communication professions, this situation, of course, is unacceptable. Kant's theory about ethical decision-making offers journalists, public relations practitioners, advertising professionals, and other communication specialists many helpful guidelines. He would want us to use reasoning to recognize ethical issues and practice virtuous behavior in our professions because it is our duty to do so. We should have the courage to think for ourselves and be fair in all our dealings, not using others as means to our ends. If communicators agree on maxims to follow—and actually follow them—the credibility of the communication professions will certainly thrive.

■ ■ ■

Baird, F. E., and W. Kaufmann. 1994. *Modern Philosophy.* Upper Saddle River, N.J.: Prentice Hall.

Baron, M. S., P. Pettit, and M. Slote. 1997. *Three Methods of Ethics.* Malden, Mass.: Blackwell Publishers.

Kant, Immanuel. 1964. *The Doctrine of Virtue: Part II of the Metaphysics of Morals.* Translated by M. J. Gregor. New York: Harper and Row. Original work published in 1797.

—————. 1981. *Grounding for the Metaphysics of Morals.* Translated by J. W. Ellington. Indianapolis: Hackett. Original work published in 1785.

—————. 1983. *Ethical Philosophy.* Translated by J. W. Ellington. Indianapolis: Hackett. Original works published in 1785/1797.

Sullivan, R. J. 1989. *Immanuel Kant's Moral Theory.* Cambridge, UK: Cambridge University Press.

Wick, Warner A. 1983. "Introduction." In Immanuel Kant, *Ethical Philosophy,* translated by J. W. Ellington. Indianapolis: Hackett.

21

Moses
Deontological Norms

WILLIAM BABCOCK

It is typical to consider one of the Old Testament's central characters, Moses, as the lawgiver who brought "God's word," the Ten Commandments or Decalogue, down from Mt. Sinai. Such a portrait of Moses as a duty-driven servant of God is accurate. However, it omits a key—if not *the* key—aspect of this biblical patriarch, and that is his humility, his meekness.

To Mount Sinai

"Now the man Moses was very meek, above all the men which were upon the face of the earth" (Numbers 12:3). Meekness signifies the eclipse of moral selfhood, and accordingly leads to the full acknowledgment of the omnipotence of God. The more Moses subdued his own self, the more he was able to magnify God, speaking with authority like a servant repeating a master's commands. As a young man, Moses' people were servants of Pharaoh. By the time he left the Israelites, the "law of the land" was not an individual, but rather the Ten Commandments. Such a transfiguration would have been impossible had Moses not subjugated a concept of self to a higher power, the deity.

As an infant Moses was protected from danger. When he was born a decree compelled the Hebrew people to cast every male child into the Nile. His mother made an ark of bulrushes or papyrus reeds, which she then made watertight with pitch, and hid it among the reeds by the river's edge. Pharaoh's daughter discovered the ark and adopted the child, educating him as an Egyptian. A power that was then unknown to Moses had protected him, and reflecting on the experience, Moses saw how the hand of God had preserved him.[1]

By the time he was grown he had received a thorough training and apparent acceptance at the Egyptian court. However, he had also observed the increasing oppression of the Israelites. He subsequently became so angered by the cruel way the Israelites were treated that in his zeal for the welfare of his people he killed an Egyptian overseer. Pharaoh heard about it, forcing Moses to flee Egypt. Rebuked by his own conscience, Moses turned away from militancy as a means of working out the salvation of his race. Realizing that his indulgence in human will had been unsuccessful, he was ready to submit to the will of God, to listen for His voice, and to obey the deity. He lived in the desert as a shepherd and eventually married a daughter of Jethro, the man who gave him a home.[2]

After forty years the Bible recounts that God appeared to Moses when he saw a desert bush in flames but not being consumed. The burning bush led Moses to his reception of a divine message, and he was also informed that God was fully aware of the problems of his people and would end their Egyptian bondage, providing them with "a good land and a large nation" (Exodus 3:8). God instructed the patriarch by means of a rod that Moses carried, and when Moses obediently threw the rod on the ground it became a serpent. When Moses, at God's command, grasped the serpent by the tail it again became a rod. And when he hid his hand in his robe and then took his hand out he found it covered with leprosy, but God showed him that it could swiftly be healed if he repeated the process. These and other signs eventually convinced the people of Moses' authority. Moses continued to meekly hesitate accepting his task, claiming to be a poor speaker, but God reminded him that the deity would teach the patriarch what to say (Exodus 4:10–16). Moses understood God's instruction asking him to return to Egypt to remind Pharaoh of the Lord's demand to "let my people go, that they may serve me" (Exodus 7:16). Pharaoh refused, the Egyptians suffered ten plagues, and Pharaoh relented and let Moses lead the Israelites from Egypt. Pharaoh changed his mind, though, pursuing the Israelites to the Red Sea. The Israelites escaped to the desert and Pharaoh's army drowned. Some

---

1. "Meekness and Might," 175.
2. Ibid., 175.

three months later the Israelites reached Mt. Sinai, where Moses the leader became Moses the lawgiver.

The Decalogue

The Bible tells us that when Moses ascended Mt. Sinai he obeyed God's call and talked with God. The patriarch learned that he needed to remind the people of the divine guidance and protection they had already received, and tell them that if they were prepared to do the will of God, that they would be God's chosen people. Moses received the Ten Commandments—or "words"—from God, and in turn he proclaimed them to the Israelites. This was logical as Moses had stood firm in the face of all the doubts and questioning of the people and their resistance both to him as leader as well as to their God.[3] Moses apparently first received the commandments orally (Exodus 20:1). He then reported them to the people, who promised to obey them. Moses then wrote down "all the words of the Lord" (Exodus 24:4). However one evaluates the Decalogue, it seems clear that it sets down basic rules of religion, morality, and human conduct that remain as valid now as in the time of Moses, the lawgiver, who was sufficiently advanced in his thinking to receive and transmit these fundamental truths for all time.[4]

As they appear in the Bible, Exodus 20:3–17, the Ten Commandments are:

1. Thou shalt have no other gods before me.
2. Thou shalt not make unto thee any graven image, or any likeness of any thing that is the heaven above, or that is in the earth beneath, or that is in the water under the earth.
3. Thou shalt not take the name of the Lord thy God in vain; for the Lord will not hold him guiltless that taketh his name in vain.
4. Remember the Sabbath day, to keep it holy.
5. Honor thy father and thy mother: that thy days may be long upon the land which the Lord thy God giveth thee.
6. Thou shalt not kill.

3. Thoma Linton Leishman, *The Continuity of the Bible: The Patriarchs*, 56.
4. Ibid., 57.

7. Thou shalt not commit adultery.

8. Thou shalt not steal.

9. Thou shalt not bear false witness against thy neighbor.

10. Thou shalt not covet thy neighbor's house, thou shalt not covet thy neighbor's wife, nor his manservant, nor his maidservant, nor his ox, nor his ass, nor any thing that is thy neighbor's.

The first five commandments concern religious and family matters that were of great importance for Israel and relate to their distinctiveness as a nation. The next four commandments are categorical prohibitions, with no punishment prescribed and no definitions given. The last commandment concerns thoughts, and is not intended to be enforced by a human judge. The Decalogue was not intended to satisfy the needs of legislator or court. Rather, it outlines a vision for the life of Israel after its liberation from Egypt. As such, it served a key function in forming the nation, and the principles it enshrines continued to be the basis of ethics for the people of God in both Old and New Testaments.[5]

Two parties entered into the covenant, or Ten Commandments: the Hebrews agreed to be faithful to Jehovah and his command, and Jehovah, through his servant, Moses, promised to be the special protector of the infant nation. The people's duties in this contract came in the form of ten "words" or short statements, likely so numbered to be easily remembered.[6]

The Decalogue has had a fundamental significance that is highlighted in different ways within the Hebrew Bible. It is not directed to any special group—priests, judges, etc.—but to the whole undifferentiated people of God. It is the direct and unmediated communication of God to Israel. The Decalogue is a statement of meaning or intention, rather than an immediate, clearly defined set of regulations. It is teaching rather than law, into which a certain order and uniformity has been brought by the attempt to mark out ten words or ten commandments in this teaching. The Decalogue is a classic statement of the life of a community of faith; it is a total statement

5. David Baker, "The Finger of God and the Forming of a Nation: The Origin and Purpose of the Decalogue," 21.

6. Albert Edward Bailey and Charles Foster Kent, *History of the Hebrew Commonwealth*, 39.

in which any part may be highlighted. Ultimately it is valued for the basic single insight it reflects: that the worship of one God implies respect for the integrity of others, and that respect for the integrity of others implies the worship of one God.[7]

The Decalogue also may be considered the Israelite constitution. It begins by stating the basis of Israel's special relationship with Yahweh, and continues to list the primary obligations laid upon her for maintenance of that relationship, including responsibilities toward both God and humankind. The Decalogue determines foundations for perpetuity, and is a charter of freedom, to be embraced and celebrated.[8]

While the Bible does not claim that Moses actually wrote the Decalogue, the narratives of Exodus and Deuteronomy, as well as subsequent tradition, make it clear that he had a major role in imparting it to Israel. The significance of the Decalogue goes far beyond the formative period of Israel's history. The ethical principles it expresses underlie the detailed laws in Exodus, Leviticus, and Deuteronomy, and served as a source of inspiration for worship, wisdom, and prophecy in ancient Israel. Since then they have had an extensive influence on law, religion, and ethics in many parts of the world and continue to do so in the present day.[9]

Moses' Deontological Foundation

Despite the miracles he had performed, the Jews did not fully believe in Moses until the event at Mt. Sinai.[10] Nevertheless, during his extended trials, Moses remained faithful to his people and to his God in leading the Israelites to the Land of Promise. He was commended for his meekness—a meekness that contained no timidity but could more appropriately be classified as selfless humility.[11] Known as a leader and lawgiver, he is also remembered as a prophet (Deuteronomy 18:15; Hosea 12:13), and he shared with Abraham the honor of being termed a friend of God (Isaiah 41:8; Exodus 33:11).

---

7. A. D. H. Mayes, "The Decalogue of Moses: An Enduring Ethical Programme?" 26, 28, 30, 39.

8. Baker, "Finger of God," 20–21.

9. Ibid., 5, 24.

10. Ben-Zion Segal, *The Ten Commandments in History and Tradition,* 87.

11. Leishman, *Continuity of the Bible,* 81.

Moses founded the religion of Israel in much the same sense that Christ Jesus founded Christianity, Muhammad founded Muhammadanism, and the Buddha founded Buddhism. While we do not call the religion of Israel Mosaism, it would be as correct to do so as it is to use names such as Christianity and Muhammadanism, and of all religion-founders, Moses likely may best be compared to Jesus and Muhammad. His work was to make tribes into a nation, united by the bond of religious law. Too, he gave to his people a practical if not yet theoretical monotheism, raising the religion of his compatriots to an ethical level and introducing into it ethical elements previously wanting.[12] Because Moses' knowledge of God was everything to him, he was loyal and obedient to what he perceived as the God of Israel.[13]

Hebrew tradition ascribes to Moses a representation of the presence of the deity in the shape of an ark or box, by which God might accompany his people. Thus the ark is a shrine of a god—Yahweh—accompanying Israel in all her movements, and through the ark the Israelites carried their God with them, that God might be omnipresent; the special deity of Israel, always in the midst of them.[14] Accordingly, the physical contents of the ark, the Ten Commandments (Deuteronomy 10) or conception of an ethical code of laws, represented the presence of God.

Moses, throughout most of his adult life, fulfilled the role of God's obedient servant; the epitome of a meek, humble individual who was duty-bound to produce, promote, and protect the word of the Lord, and thus perpetuate the deity itself for all time and peoples.

■　■　■

Alexander, Pat, ed. 1978. *The Lion Encyclopedia of the Bible.* Sydney: Lion Publishing Corporation.

Bailey, Albert Edward, and Charles Foster Kent. 1949. *History of the Hebrew Commonwealth.* New York: Charles Scribner's Sons.

Baker, David. 2005. "The Finger of God and the Forming of a Nation: The Origin and Purpose of the Decalogue." *Tyndale Bulletin* 56, no. 1: 1–25.

12. John P. Peters, "The Religion of Moses," 104–5.
13. Samuel Greenwood, *Footsteps of Israel: From Eden to the City of God,* 85.
14. Peters, "Religion of Moses," 111–12.

Greenwood, Samuel. 1944. *Footsteps of Israel: From Eden to the City of God.* Boston: A. A. Beauchamp.

Holy Bible. 1968. Authorized King James Version. Grand Rapids, Mich.: Zondervan Publishing House.

Hyatt, James Philip. 1965. "Moses and the Ethical Decalogue." *Encounter* 26, no. 2: 199–206.

Leishman, Thomas Linton. 1968. *The Continuity of the Bible: The Patriarchs.* Boston: Christian Science Publishing Society.

Mayes, A. D. H. 1991. "The Decalogue of Moses: An Enduring Ethical Programme?" In *Ethics and the Christian,* 25–40. Dublin: Columba Press.

"Meekness and Might." 1950. *Christian Science Journal* 68, no. 4: 175–76.

Peters, John P. 1901. "The Religion of Moses." *Journal of Biblical Literature* 20, no. 2: 101–28.

Segal, Ben-Zion. 1990. *The Ten Commandments in History and Tradition.* Hebrew University of Jerusalem: Magnes Press.

22

Thomas Hobbes
The Ethics of Social Order

STEPHEN J. A. WARD

When Thomas Hobbes fled from London to Paris in 1640 to escape persecution, he was, as he later wrote, "the first of all that fled" (Martinich 2005, 3). In *Leviathan,* Hobbes, who described himself as a "timid" man, claimed that his only aim was to present some useful, impartial, truths "occasioned by the disorders of the present time."

Hobbes, however, was neither timid nor impartial. Writing about politics in the seventeenth century was by itself an act of courage, inviting attack. Nor were his "truths" modest. Hobbes advanced a bold thesis that entangled him in the disputes of his time: humans can only enjoy peaceful society if they agree to be ruled by a powerful sovereign who prevents society from sliding into a state of war. Power is legitimized and peace obtained through a social contract between citizens and sovereign.

Hobbes's blunt assertions about men as power-seekers and his support for powerful sovereignty offended contemporaries. Even today, Hobbes is regarded in some quarters as a conservative curmudgeon, cynical of human nature. People recall his famous line about life being "nasty, brutish, and short," ignoring that he was talking about a state of war. Or they cite his claim that men's desires lead to conflict, ignoring his view that men's desires (and reason) also incline them toward peace. Even solid books on Hobbes today have jacket covers that state incorrectly that Hobbes believed men only acted selfishly. Some argue that Hobbes's philosophy is a realpolitik analysis of power, not an ethical theory.

Hobbes's Life

A correction of this cramped view of Hobbes starts with a review of his life, as he progressed from humanist to scientist and philosopher, and finally to the controversial author of *Leviathan*. Hobbes was born into a modest family at Malmesbury, Wiltshire, in 1588, the year of the Spanish Armada. His father, Thomas, was a drunken minor clergyman who abandoned his family. Luckily, Hobbes had an uncle, a successful glover, who sent the intellectually precocious Hobbes to Oxford, where he excelled in Renaissance studies and languages, and was bored by Aristotelianism.

His first work, in 1628, was a translation of Thucydides, a skeptic of Athenian democracy. Upon graduation, he became tutor to the eldest son of William Cavendish of Hardwick, the Earl of Devonshire, an association that would last a lifetime. One of his duties was to take the heirs to earldoms on the Grand Tour of Europe. Hobbes thereby gained access to the political and intellectual elites across Europe. During this period, Hobbes developed a deep interest in geometry and the new mechanical science of Galileo. In 1640, Hobbes wrote the first of several versions of his political theory, *The Elements of Law, Natural and Politic.* This book of "infallible rules and true science of justice and equity" supported Charles I at a time when Parliament was questioning the king's power. Into this life of intellectual and cultural stimulation, the English civil war intervened. Hobbes, fearing for his safety, fled to Paris for eleven years, where he became mathematics tutor to Charles II, also in exile.

As the English civil war moved toward regicide, Hobbes, in Paris, began writing *Leviathan,* the authoritative presentation of his theory of sovereignty. He published it in 1651, two years after Charles I was beheaded, to a strong and often negative reception in England and France. Nevertheless, Hobbes, now in his early sixties, decided to return to England. Throughout the 1650s, Hobbes was safe and famous in England, and he could teach his ideas at gatherings. But his irascible personality was not suited for polite conversation. A seventeenth-century biographer of Hobbes wrote: "If anyone objected against his dictates, he would leave the company in a passion, saying, his business was to teach. Not dispute" (Martinich 2005, 150).

The 1660s ushered in a difficult final period of his life, as leading Establishment figures attacked Hobbes's ideas. Hobbes became embroiled in disputations with clergymen, scientists, and politicians. Clergy suspected that Hobbes's materialism implied atheism and they bristled at his view that the sovereign should control religion. In scientific circles, Hobbes was not popular. He was irritated when he was not asked to be a member of London's Royal Society, partly because he didn't believe strongly in experimentation. But his personality had something to do with it. Robert Hooke confessed that he could not bear Hobbes's tendency to "undervalue all other men's opinions." Meanwhile, the attacks continued. In 1666, the House of Commons named *Leviathan* as a heretical book. Hobbes burned some of his papers to protect himself. In 1683, Oxford University condemned *Leviathan* for claiming that self-preservation "supercedes the obligation of all others." Growing old and tired of the controversies, Hobbes reduced his publishing. By the mid-1670s, he left London and spent most of his final years on the estate of the Earl of Devonshire. But he was not idle. Hobbes translated into English both the *Odyssey* and *Iliad* of Homer before he died on December 4, 1679, after a long illness. He was buried near Hardwick Hall in Derbyshire.

Hobbes's Ideas

One theme unifies Hobbes's life and work: the search for something secure in an uncertain world. In his personal life, Hobbes sought recognition as he ascended England's hierarchy from the son of a cleric to a friend of Francis Bacon and a disputant with Rene Descartes. Intellectually, Hobbes sought necessary knowledge of humans through the deductive methods of geometry and scientific ideas. Politically, Hobbes sought to erect a new science of politics with secure truths about proper government. His search for security is understandable. Hobbes lived through the savage Thirty Years War and then watched his country devolve into a civil war that ended with the shocking execution of Charles I. Twenty years later, the unstable English republic restored the Stuarts. For Hobbes, citizens needed lessons in obedience and peacekeeping.

Hobbes' *Leviathan* seeks a rational basis for a firm social order. His political conclusions are the top of a pyramid that sits upon four fundamental premises: (1) Mechanical materialism—all things are explained by matter in motion. (2) Psychological egoism—humans, by nature, seek power to satisfy their desires. (3) Ethical relativity—good is relative to what humans find desirable. Duties are relative to contracts. (4) Ethics is reducible to rationality—norms are justified if they serve the rational interests of individuals.

Leviathan opens with chapters on the nature of man as a mechanical apparatus of sense organs, desires, nerves, and muscles that respond to external bodies. Desires and aversions are the main sources of movement. In voluntary actions, we deliberate about (or calculate) the means of achieving a desired object or avoiding an undesired object. Whatever object is desired by a man is "for his part calleth *Good*." Conversely, the object of a man's "Hate, and Aversion" is "*Evil*" (1985, chapter 6). All humans have a fundamental impulse to keep moving, to satisfy desires, and to avoid death. Desires in humans are incessant and continually changing. Different humans desire different things in different degrees, from riches to pleasure. Hobbes defines "power" as a man's "present means, to obtain some future apparent good" (1985, chapters 10–11).

So far, Hobbes's psychology does not appear to be particularly troublesome. Men *are* desirous creatures that seek their good. It does not follow that humans are selfish by nature because the interests of others could be among the desires of individuals. Every human must seek some power, but not all will maximize their power. So, ethically speaking, where does the trouble begin? It begins when Hobbes moves from an analysis of the individual to that of society. If men are primarily atomic units of desire-satisfaction and power-seeking, then human interaction is primarily the dynamics of how humans obtain, increase, negotiate, and limit power. When humans, as units of desire-satisfaction, live together they come into tension and competition. In a social setting, the power of any individual is qualified by the power of other individuals. More importantly, some men's desires are without limit, and we can never be sure who such men are. We can never be sure that by acting moderately we will not be robbed of the means to satisfy our desires. Faced with this insecurity, even humans with moderate desires must engage in power struggles to be sure they won't be prey for immoderate humans who conceal their ambitions (1985, chapter 11).

For Hobbes, this power struggle happens not because men are innately evil, immoderate, or irrational. Nor is Hobbes praising the pursuit of power. The exercise of power is a fact of life and, in society, people fall into destructive conflicts because of a lack of assurance about other people. What is lacking is a system of social order that assures humans it is safe to live moderately and abide by agreements. Hobbes is warning that beneath any social order lurks this reality of power struggles. Government must be designed to recognize and address this underlying threat to peace.

What sort of government can establish a firm social order? At this point, Hobbes engages in a popular seventeenth-century thought experiment. He considers the origins of society by imagining a hypothetical state of nature without government. Hobbes argues that in a state of nature, humans devolve into a state of war for the same reasons of doubt and insecurity noted previously. In a state of nature, all men have an unlimited "Right of Nature" to do whatever they think best to preserve themselves. But as long as men exercise this right, there can be no security for anyone. A state of nature is a state of war (1985, chapter 14). Men, therefore, are disposed to seek "Articles of Peace" by contract with other men by virtue of their reason, their fear of death and domination, and their desire for "commodious living." Escaping the state of nature requires that humans agree to a social contract where humans "transfer" their right of nature to a sovereign who has the power to secure the peace and allow civilized society to exist. Only when such a contract is established do men come under anything called "duty" or "justice."

For Hobbes, there must be one supreme sovereign or *Leviathan* (or "Mortal God") who is given the power to maintain peace, enforce contracts, and punish men of immoderate desires. This sovereign may be one man or an assembly of men. The sovereign must have authority over what is published and communicated, over religion, and over what is judged right and good since these are matters that may disturb the peace. Yet the people do not owe obedience to a sovereign who breaks the contract or who cannot assure their safety. Hobbes thinks his political structure provides an adequate framework within which humans can safely pursue their goods.

What, in the end, was Hobbes proposing to his contemporaries? He was not suggesting literally that they make a social contract. Nor did he think that a state of nature had ever existed, although he thinks that the civil wars and "savage peoples" of his time approach a state of nature. Hobbes used the state-of-nature device to encourage contemporaries to pledge obedience to a powerful sovereign, or risk going back to civil and religious wars. He wanted to show that obedience could be based not on the divine right of kings but on a social contract that served the rational advantage of citizens.

Hobbes's Legacy

What is Hobbes's legacy for today's ethical and political theory, once we have eliminated obvious misunderstandings? Historically, Hobbes is the first great English philosopher and political scientist of modern times. Hobbes and Locke, despite their differences, stand at the head of an ever-widening stream of contract thought that would provide a basis for today's liberalism. Hobbes addresses questions of special relevance to our world: What is the legitimate basis for the use of power? How is peace possible, given the nature of humans and current conditions?

Ethically, Hobbes is the grandfather of modern naturalism and relativism in ethics. Naturalism holds that ethical values are to be understood by appeal only to the natural conditions of humans. Ethical philosophy, from Hobbes and Locke to Hume and Kant, sought to ground ethics in desire, pleasure, reason, or moral sentiments. Hobbes, in defining "good" and "duty" as relative to desires and contracts, respectively, provides an early explanation of how norms are human constructs.

Yet we should not read Hobbes uncritically. His mechanical materialism and psychology are out-of-date, and he does not pay adequate attention to the social identity of humans. His project to derive norms solely from rationality is dubious. A society held together only by individual advantage lacks the bonds to be a stable, just society. Also, Hobbes's contractualism is an insufficient basis for the construction of a society that is not only peaceful and efficient but also egalitarian and just, in a modern liberal sense. Once Hobbes's sovereign is established theoretically, one still does not know what the contract implies about the just organization of social institutions, the status and treatment of the disadvantaged, and the fair distribution of the advantages of social cooperation among all citizens. Finally, Hobbes's idea of a Leviathan runs against a liberal optimism about the potentiality of humans and a democratic temperament.

Ultimately, we should see Hobbes as an important historical figure who expressed seminal ideas that developed into different traditions.

As in theory, so he was in life—a complicated, fascinating figure: a materialist who was a practicing Anglican; a theorist who was neither a royalist who believed in the divine right of kings nor a democrat; a theorist of "absolute sovereignty" yet a "liberal" who helped formulate the idea of the rights of humans.

Every serious student of ethics needs to engage Hobbes's philosophy to determine, for themselves, where he erred, where they disagree, and where we need to do better today.

■ ■ ■

Hobbes, Thomas. 1839–1845. *The English Works of Thomas Hobbes.* 11 vols. Edited by William Molesworth. London: J. Bohn.

———. 1985. *Leviathan.* Edited by C. B. MacPherson. London: Penguin Classics.

Martinich, Aloysius P. 2005. *Hobbes.* New York and London: Routledge.

Sorell, Thomas, ed. 1996. *Cambridge Companion to Hobbes.* Cambridge, UK: Cambridge University Press.

The Communitarian Stance
Loyalty to the Community

This stance is closest to what is typically known as social ethics.

Communitarian ethics places a major emphasis on the idea of democracy, is committed to public conversation and cooperation, and seeks consensus. This is an ethics of the common good; whatever is ethical supports and expands the community.

Thinkers who promote communitarian ethics express this communal concern in different ways: Confucius stresses family and group loyalty and following community rituals. Gandhi advocates nonviolent group action. Marx breaks through class differences. Dewey highlights the pragmatic group concerns for expanding education and democracy. Habermas advocates knowledgeable dialogue that benefits the whole by involving the people themselves in their own decision-making. Levinas contributes to this perspective by making the well-being of others within the community the basic standard for ethics.

PART V

Confucius
Ethics of Character

VIRGINIA WHITEHOUSE

Confucius had a lot to say about ethics and communication. To consider his ideas in relation to modern Western, particularly American, thought, we have to start by understanding that he was a great man living in ancient China and trying to emulate and revive the customs of an even earlier era. He believed the morals of his people were on a rapid decline because the expectations for civility, traditional rites, and respect for societal roles were waning. He maintained that people can be ethical if they practice key virtues that are best lived out in understanding of their place in their community. Therefore his philosophies are the appropriate place to begin a modern consideration of communitarian ethics.

K'ung Ch'iu (551–479 BCE) was born to a noble family that had fallen on hard financial times. More than two thousand years later Jesuit missionaries translated his name and title of teacher, K'ung Fu-tzu, together as Confucius. At key points in Chinese history, some worshiped the scholar as a god. Legend relays that a unicorn appeared with a jade tablet in his mouth prophesying Confucius' birth. More frequently, however, he is honored not as a deity but as China's greatest philosopher. What we do know about his early life is that his father had been a magistrate and a noted warrior, but died when Confucius was three years old. His mother struggled to raise him in poverty but died in his youth. Despite these losses, Confucius was widely considered to be among the best-educated men of his time. By age twenty-two he established what was arguably the first private school, a century before Socrates. He was the Renaissance man of his generation, a millenium before Europe took to the concept. He sought a thoroughly liberal education grounded in everything from history, literature, politics, and music—particularly the five-string lute—to archery, horsemanship, calligraphy, mathematics, and, most significantly here, ethics. Due to his financial straits, he had to take a number of jobs deemed lowly for a scholar but necessary to support his family, including overseeing fields and a granary. He garnered a reputation for working hard and showing respect for all, regardless of the status of the job. Throughout his life he held some government appointments. Eventually appointed prime minister of his native state of Lu, Confucius reportedly eliminated crime, restored order, and gained the respect of the people within months. He resigned in disgust when the ruling duke fell to corruption and carousing. Then he spent years traveling, learning, and gaining wide respect for his teaching.

Interestingly enough, Confucius' lifetime overlaps with Siddhartha Gautama (563–483 BCE), known as the Buddha, whose teachings also had great influence and at times competed with Confucian thought throughout China. The sixth century BCE is at times referred as the "great century" because Confucius, Buddha, Mahavira (the Jain) and Lao Tzu (the Taoist) lived and spread their ideas. This period launched the Classical Era in China where it is said that "One Hundred Schools of Thought" (a figurative rather than literal phrase) competed for dominance of philosophical influence, and Confucianism was a leading player.

The Confucian canon includes the Six Classics, which are works Confucius studied and possibly edited, and the Four Books, which outline Confucius' own key teachings. Most are dialogues and messages documented after his death, much as Jesus' conversations with disciplines were included in the Bible or as Socrates' dialogues were recorded by Plato. Of the Four Books, scholars believe that one of Confucius' most devoted students wrote *The Great Learning* (also translated as *Great Wisdom*) while Confucius' grandson wrote *The Doctrine of the Mean* (also translated as *Genuine Living*). Mencius studied with that grandson's disciples and is believed to have written the book titled aptly *Mencius*. The *Analects* (also translated as *Collected Sayings*) is the most famous of the Four Books. Like the others, the *Analects* can be confusing because they read like a series of one-liners and disconnected conversations. But within these repetitious passages is powerful wisdom about ethics, relationships, and action:

Do not be concerned about others appreciating you. Be concerned about your not appreciating others. (Book 2, Verse 16)

To know what is right and not to do it is to be without courage. (Book 2, Verse 24)

A man who has virtue is sure to have something to say. A man who has something to say is not sure to have virtue. A man who has benevolence is sure to have courage. A man who has courage is not sure to have benevolence. (Book 14, Verse 4)

Across the centuries, many embraced, rejected, and then embraced again Confucius' ideals. The Four Books and related commentaries served as the foundation for the Chinese imperial civil service examinations during the last three hundred years of the examination system until 1905.

Accounts describe Confucius as highly dignified, graceful, eloquent, firm, and compassionate. The *Analects* reports, "Confucius was gentle yet strict, awe-inspiring yet not fearful, and courteous yet at ease" (Book 7, Verse 38). That is exactly what his teachings advocate a gentleman, scholar, and leader should be. He believed that the family was the cornerstone of society. For the family to work effectively, each member must live out his or her roles well, with civility and grace. If the family roles are in order, then the rest of society should function harmoniously. In the *Analects*, Confucius states: "Let the lords be lords, the subjects be subjects, the fathers be fathers, and the sons be sons" (Chapter 12, Verse 11). Five key relationships are identified in his works: ruler and subject; father and son; husband and wife; older and younger brother; and relations between friends, the only equal relationship. Other relationships, such as business owner to worker, would be implied from these foundations. The senior owes the junior protection and consideration for well-being. The junior owes the senior obedience and respect.

From these relationships, we get the Confucian version of the Golden Rule and reciprocity: a son should treat his father the way he would want to be treated if he were the father. The son should treat the father with utmost respect, even if he believes the father is making poor choices, because of the status inherent in the father's role. To cast this teaching in the negative format attributed to Confucius: don't impose on others what you would not want imposed on you. The negative language is of particular interest to intercultural communicators because this approach can help avoid cultural imperialism. The negative voice reflects a strong preference among Taoists to avoid meddling in others' affairs. To act upon someone else, as stated in the Golden Rule, would be perceived as highly unethical and intrusive. However, to not act, to not impose, would be appropriate. Therefore, Confucius certainly is a product of and influence upon a collectivist and even a communitarian society, but the foundation is deferential rather than egalitarian. In modern Asian cultures, communication tends to occur to define relationships. These unequal relationships function through reciprocal obligations that must be met in prescribed ways. Rites may be different today in Singapore, China, South Korea, or Japan, but the nature of the relationship and the necessity of ritual are all founded in Confucian ideals. That means not everyone has the right to speak at all times. The highest-ranking person has both the greatest authority and the greatest responsibility.

Confucius defined a key concept of interest for communitarians: *Jen*, which is translated as good will, benevolence, or acting for the good of society. An ordered society is filled with people who act in good will for others by living out their roles. Confucius said *jen* means to love others. Benevolence (*jen*), along with propriety (*li*) and righteousness or faithfulness (*yi*), are virtues that could be developed by all people. Later scholars added wisdom (*zhi*) and sincerity (*hsin*) to create the Five Constant Virtues. These virtues, as with Aristotle's virtues, can be learned. Confucius believed the Rites, or traditions and ceremonies, were the best way to practice and learn virtue. One could not be achieved without the other. Rites are the outward evidence of solid internal character. The specifics of these rites are not specified, but repeated reference is made to *Tian* or Heaven, while he also warns against spirits. Ancestors should be honored in the way the ancestors would wish. Most scholars would call Confucius a deist of sorts.

Just as Confucius offered versions of reciprocity that would have pleased Kant and versions of virtue that coincided with Aristotle, he also introduced The Way, which he frames similarly to Natural Law. Heaven created moral order just as Heaven set the physical order into motion, Confucius believed. Doing right should occur not merely because of the authority of Heaven or because doing right will bring good results. The gentleman scholar should do good because good is the right thing to do. The Way requires the scholar to pursue learning, embrace traditions, cultivate virtue, and engage in public service. By setting the virtuous example and keeping his family functional and harmonious, the scholar has done his part in keeping society in order.

In the centuries following his death, a range of interpretations and Confucian schools of thought emerged and clashed, particularly about human nature. Hsuntzu adopted a more teleological or what has come to be called "realistic" interpretation. People, he argued, are basically evil and corrupted by greed. Hsuntzu dismissed the idea that morality is innate and could be released through learning. Instead, he believed government must serve as a humane but strict moral compass and punish wrongdoers severely; the state served as the moral enforcer.

Mo-tzu, also a teleologist, focused on a different and more optimistic strain of thought: everyone should be loved and treated equally, regardless of whether they are enemy, inside one's own family, or a neighboring family. This he said would lead to good consequences and Heaven would smile on the arrangement.

Mencius, a most influential idealist and deontologist, believed that Mo-tzu was impractical because one has different obligations to family and strangers. At the same time, he found Mo-tzu's ideas corrupting. Principles should be followed because following a principle is good; fear of Heaven's wrath and other negative consequences should have nothing to do with it. Nonetheless, Mencius also believed people are basically good and universal moral law lay within humanity, given from Heaven. In *Mencius*, Kao Tzu and Mencius debate the question of innate goodness:

> Kao Tzu said, "Human nature is like whirling water. Give it an outlet in the east and it will flow east; give it an outlet in the west and it will flow west . . . "
> "It certainly is the case," said Mencius, "that water does not show any preference for either east or west, but does it show the same indifference to high and low? Human nature is good just as water seeks low *ground*. There is no man who is not good; there is no water that does not flow downwards." (Book VI)

The more a person studied, Mencius believed, the clearer universal moral law would become. Virtue is like a seed inside each person and learning is the sun, rain, and good soil that allow the seed to grow. Certainly drought and flood, ignorance and lack of opportunity, can kill the seed, but the seed nonetheless is present. Confucius defined what he believed to be an ideal way of living, working, and governing; Mencius created a workable defense of Confucian ethics.

Perhaps the greatest admonition Confucius would give modern communicators is that even possessing all the technology in the world does not negate the value of a broad-based liberal arts education; of treating others, particularly superiors, with respect; and of general civility. The more one practices civility and the Constant Virtues, the more good becomes ingrained in that person's life. Communitarians would embrace Confucius' assertion that public service is the means by which one lives out those virtues.

■ ■ ■

Bahm, Archie J. 1993. *The Heart of Confucius: Interpretations of "Genuine Living" and "Great Wisdom."* Fremont, Calif.: Jain Publishing Company.

Baird, Forrest, and Raeburn Heimbeck. 2006. *Asian Philosophy.* Upper Saddle River, N.J.: Pearson.

Confucius. 1993. *The Analects.* Translated and edited by Raymond Dawson. Oxford, UK: Oxford University Press.

———. 1996. *Lun Yu.* Translated by William Cheung. Hong Kong: Confucian Press.

Mencius. 1970. Translated by D. C. Lau. London: Penguin.

24

Mohandas Gandhi
Fellowship of Power

LEE WILKINS

Gandhi, as perhaps no other leader, epitomizes the concept that ethics is not something one has, ethics is something one does. For Gandhi, the two were one. "I am told that religion and politics are different spheres of life. But I would say without a moment's hesitation and yet in all modesty that those who claim this do not know what religion is."[1]

The ancient Greeks viewed politics as the highest ethical activity. Only in the exercise of politics did human beings flourish in a community with their fellows. What connected politics, religion, and ethics for Gandhi was power. But, it was power of a particular sort that Gandhi sought to understand, acquire, and redistribute in a way that redressed what he believed were the most essential problems of his home: the violence to human dignity that only abject poverty can produce and the deleterious impact of the rigid caste system on community. Power, for Gandhi, was what political theorist James C. Davies has labeled an instrumental need (Davies 1964): without power, it is impossible to exercise autonomy, to form relationships, and to nurture community. Through the exercise of power, one comes to know oneself. During his lifetime, Gandhi argued through his actions that journalists were powerful people, employed by powerful institutions whose actions must be informed by a duty to human kind. Gandhi sought the power of transformation: the ability through action to help himself and his followers reshape themselves and their world into a more just, more caring place.

1. E. H. Erikson, *Gandhi's Truth: On the Origins of Militant Non-Violence*, 22.

Mohandas K. Gandhi (the surname Gandhi literally means "gro-
cer") was the youngest child of a "young mother (25) and an aging
father (47)".[2] He spent the first decade of his life in the port city of
Porbandar on the coast of the Arabian Sea. He shared a house with
his father, his five brothers, and their families; six generations of
Gandhis were home ministers or prime ministers. Gandhi's mother,
Putali Ba, has been described as the ideal housewife, but the somewhat communal living arrangements of this very large household
meant that "Western" constructions of male and female roles were
more fungible than the contemporary meaning of the word "housewife" might suggest. Gandhi's identification with his mother and
his mother's work foreshadows his campaigns to elevate women's
status in India and to redistribute both the daily work of women
and men—and hence their power in the home and in the community—to a more equal plane. Some biographers have credited
Putali Ba's religious bent with Gandhi's tactic of fasting at pivotal
moments. While this interpretation of his mother's influence is in
some dispute, it is at least as important to understand that Putali
Ba belonged to a small religious sect that prided itself on having unified the Qur'an with the Hindu scriptures and rejected any attempt
of one to supersede the other. From his earliest religious training,
Gandhi understood that the politics of religion—or at least the dog-
ma of religion—was in itself a battle for supremacy. To resist such a
struggle was both a political and a religious act. Putali Ba's religion
also prepared the young boy "for the refusal to take anybody's word
for what anything meant, either in the Hindu scriptures which he
rediscovered only in his youth with the help of Western writings, or
in the Christians gospels, the essence of which he tried to resurrect in
Eastern and modern terms."[3]

From his father the young boy learned the daily art of political
statecraft. His father, whom Gandhi called Kaba, was the administra-
tor of one of the Kathiawar princes (a sort of prime minister's court)
that was held daily in Gandhi's home. Kaba held this post throughout
Gandhi's childhood. When the boy was about ten, his father took a
more lucrative and powerful role as the prime minister in Rajkot, a
change that jeopardized both Kaba's career and his health. After what
must have been a difficult two years, Kaba quit this new post, but not

2. Ibid., 103.
3. Ibid., 112.

before his employer reminded Kaba that he could use the money he would have earned to send his intellectually gifted youngest son to England to study. The next set of facts upon which most biographers agree is Gandhi's contracted marriage, at the age of thirteen. The ceremony was combined with that of an older brother and a nephew. It was contracted in this way not merely for financial considerations but so that Kaba could be present. Erikson's biography, which is quite psychoanalytic, notes that after his marriage, Gandhi took an increasingly responsible role in the extended household, caring for his ailing father, helping his mother, and, at the same time, being a husband to his wife. Most biographies mention that Gandhi left his father's deathbed to have sexual relations with his wife. The adult Gandhi sharply criticized his father for the marriage and the way it occurred; Erikson views the father-son relationship as the kiln from which Gandhi's adult embrace of *ahimsa*, a quality of all encompassing, transforming love, emerged.

This review of Gandhi's childhood influences might suggest that his fusion of politics and ethics was merely the adult working out of patterns established much earlier. Such was not the case. Even in his earliest years, Gandhi was a "special" child, preoccupied with questions of ethics and with a vision of solving problems in ways that ignored previously accepted and established dichotomies. In his examination of *Extraordinary Minds*, psychologist Howard Gardner creates a special category for Gandhi, the influencer, who through a life well lived literally embodies "the creation of a narrative in which they make a common bond with their followers; by describing goals they seek in common, obstacles that lie in the way, measures for dealing with these obstacles, milestones along the way, and the promise that the desired utopia can eventually be achieved."[4] Gandhi's life narrative, drenched as it was in equal measures of empathy and purpose, reminds both journalists and advertising practitioners of the power of narrative to transform how audiences see themselves, others, and their communities. Furthermore, such a story—with the "plot points" that Gardner notes—is far more likely to provide audiences with the sort of insight that allows them to function simultaneously as autonomous individuals and collectively as members of the human family. The narrative Gandhi would suggest, particularly for

4. H. Gardner, *Extraordinary Minds: Portraits of Four Exceptional Individuals and an Examination of Our Own Extraordinariness*, 108.

news, is not one laced with recurring episodes of conflict unresolved. "Conflicts need not entail violence—they can proceed by a logic that makes both parties feel legitimate, even ennobled. This was a new, more inclusive story—one in which onetime rivals suppressed their difference in favor of a joint pursuit."[5]

Gandhi began this work of uniting differences in his young adulthood, when he left India to study law in England. When he returned home, he learned of his mother's death. During this time in England, the twenty-something student described himself as awkward and often out of place. Gandhi viewed himself as not a particularly able intellectual, but rather a gifted student of the human heart. His subsequent career reflected the theoretically deep knowledge of the ethical and political linchpins of representative democracy that emerged from his British legal education. He returned to India in 1891, but soon set out for South Africa, where he would begin his lifelong task of reminding the British Empire that the ethical foundations on which its democracy was built rejected slavery, human servitude, and the political dominion of the powerful over the colonial. Indeed, when confronted with this ethical and political fact, admittedly over a series of decades, the British, having themselves been transformed by the conversation, left India not as demons or as whipped curs, but as friends.

Gandhi's concept of role, in which the change agent himself becomes changed by a dialogue among equals, has implications for both advertising practitioners and public relations professionals, each of whom seek to influence both public opinion and action. Professional practice that values equality, is willing to be changed by the conversation with the audience, and has the goal of acting *with* as opposed to acting *upon,* would encourage strategic communication professionals to put an audience's genuine needs first, and sales second. In this reorientation, credibility, trust, and hence sales would flourish for the long term. Gandhi's concept of self as audience, for example, would support advertising campaigns such as Dove's campaign for real beauty or public relations efforts that place advocacy for the good of the community on an equal footing with advocacy for the client alone.

Gandhi is best known for what Americans have termed "political nonviolence" or "passive resistance." Both of these phrases are accu-

5. Ibid., 109.

rate descriptions of tactics (peaceful protests, such as the Civil Rights marches of the early 1960s or the contemporary marches against the U.S.-led invasion of Iraq). But they fail to capture some of the deeper meanings of *satyagraha,* which more closely translated means the power or force of truth, nonviolence, and love. The fact that these concepts (and their articulation as political tactics) have the power to transform and transcend the individual who practices them and the society in which they are employed was Gandhi's larger, ethically informed end. In the American vernacular, "passive" often connotes weakness. For Gandhi, passive meant provocative, and he believed that such a response was best employed on society's most difficult problems. One of his students remarked:

> Nonviolence, he said with a deep and, I felt, somewhat tragic pensiveness, will be the weapon of choice wherever democracy itself has made issues so opaque and complex that a return to an utter simplicity of approach becomes mandatory—as is the case now with your country [i.e., the U.S. in the 1960s].[6]

Those who practiced *satyagraha* did so through *swaraj,* which means freedom in two distinct senses—"external" freedom or political independence, and "internal" freedom, a concept derived from Buddhist and Hindu thought that means spiritual liberation achieved through psychological freedom from fear, ignorance, and illusion. Thomas Mann captures this definition in his short story "Mario and the Magician" (Mann 1989), his fictional portrait of Mussolini whom the peasant, Mario, through great struggle and pain, repudiates. Gandhi's truth was a faith in the power of hope to generate change in the human spirit and hence in human action. Gandhi's truth was neither naive nor saccharine; he understood that the most difficult thing to change is the human heart, that people must live change in order to internalize it, that living change requires community, and that the process of change is marred by mistakes as well as marked by success. In order to convey this narrative, Gandhi used the media of his day, newspapers, at least one of which was outlawed by the British in India as seditious. Gandhi said that, in order to build community, one needs a journal. In his thinking, then, journalism was a very important profession. Vince Walker of the *New York Times* won a Pulitzer for his coverage of Gandhi; one of Margaret Bourke-

6. Erikson, *Gandhi's Truth,* 85.

White's most memorable photo essays for *Life* magazine was of an imprisoned Gandhi during World War II. Gandhi's wife died during this imprisonment, which she shared with him as she shared all of his significant political and social work.

Gandhi never held elected political office in India. But, he is considered the father of that country, and his influence today is global. Martin Luther King invoked Gandhi during the Civil Rights marches and demonstrations of the late 1950s and early 1960s. At home, Gandhi continued to nurture his country by helping mentor, in politics and ethics, the generation of leaders who governed India during its early independence. Gandhi believed that this sort of mentorship was a highly moral act and the responsibility of every leader. Autobiographies of those whom Gandhi touched in this way provide evidence of the Mahatma's (Hindi for "great soul") lasting, personal impact. As Indian independence drew near, Gandhi also realized that the new nation would have severe religious divisions that would threaten its immediate and long-term future. Gandhi, more than any other leader of his time, worked directly with India's Islamic citizens to attempt to heal this religious breach. That he was unsuccessful in this effort led both to the founding of Pakistan and to his assassination.

How might journalists apply the insights of *satyagraha* to their daily work, something Gandhi believed was essential and which he acknowledged could often be routine and petty? One clear way would be to employ the concepts of fear, ignorance, and illusion as an alternative definition of news, and to report extensively on elements in society where these corrosive outlooks hold sway. For example, Gandhi would have applauded increased attention to urban poverty, both before and after Hurricane Katrina made it so visible in New Orleans in 2005. Equally, Gandhi would have recommended the same guidelines for how to treat sources, editors, and colleagues. News articles that eschew violence would, by necessity, invade privacy less frequently. They would hold the powerful to truthful account, including investigative reporting, extensive coverage of politics and economics, and more thoughtful attention to social movements. Gandhi would have applauded the long-form journalistic narrative, whether in the hands of journalistic greats such as Edward R. Murrow or in contemporary personality profiles of "people who make a difference" on the network news. And, he certainly would have had a special regard for the political communication of Jon Stewart, whose humor (without mockery) better punctures illusion than more straightforward, traditional reporting.

In all of this, Gandhi would have found, and in his own life demonstrated, the power of journalism which seeks, however incrementally, to transform political society into a just democracy informed by care. This vision speaks to journalistic role and to concrete decisions equally. Although it is highly aspirational in nature, Gandhi's life demonstrated that aspiration and generativity have the power to change much for the better. He would have expected that journalists would understand—and practice this understanding of truth—as well.

■ ■ ■

Brown, J. 1989. *Gandhi: Prisoner of Hope.* New Haven, Conn.: Yale University Press.

Dalton, D. 1993. *Mahatma Gandhi: Nonviolent Power in Action.* New York: Columbia University Press.

Davies, James C. 1964. *Human Nature in Politics.* New York: John Wiley and Sons.

Erikson, E. H. 1969. *Gandhi's Truth: On the Origins of Militant Nonviolence.* New York: W. W. Norton and Co.

Gandhi. 1982. Multiple formats. Directed by Richard Attenborough. Los Angeles: Columbia Pictures.

Gardner, H. 1997. *Extraordinary Minds: Portraits of Four Exceptional Individuals and an Examination of Our Own Extraordinariness.* New York: Basic Books.

Mann, Thomas. 1989. "Mario and the Magician." In *Death in Venice and Seven Other Stories.* New York: Vintage.

25

Karl Marx
Transcending Alienation

JON BEKKEN

Perhaps the most influential social thinker of the nineteenth century, Karl Marx (1818–1883) was born into an era of social ferment. The age of industrialization was underway, creating both enormous fortunes and widespread privation across Europe. A new social stratum of intellectuals, professionals, and other educated men formed an emerging public sphere, challenging existing traditions in every domain. The Enlightenment revolutionized philosophy with its celebration of reason and progress. Popular demands for democratization and rationalization challenged monarchical power across Europe, ultimately leading to the formation of the modern nation state and the emergence of civil society as a countervailing power. Marx was both a product of and a participant in this social ferment, and remains one of the most influential philosophers and social critics of all time.

The son of a moderately prosperous Jewish lawyer who was forced to convert to the state church when Prussia annexed the Rhineland, Karl Marx studied philosophy and law at the Universities of Berlin and Jena. When his radicalism made a career as an academic impossible, Marx became editor of a new liberal newspaper in Cologne, a center of German radicalism. When it was suppressed in 1843, Marx and his new wife were forced into exile. He briefly returned to Cologne during the 1848 revolution to edit the *Neue Rheinische Zeitung*, was tried for sedition when royal authority was reestablished, and was expelled from the country after his acquittal. Marx would spend the rest of his life in exile, mostly in England.

Aside from his writings for the *New York Tribune* and other news-papers, which afforded at best a meager livelihood, Marx spent the remainder of his life developing his critique of capitalism, and working to build an international socialist movement that rejected more utopian traditions in favor of what he saw as a sound, scientific approach. Influential but also controversial in radical circles, Marx played a key role in the rise of the International Workingmen's Association—an association of European unionists and socialists that sought to develop workers' solidarity and coordination across the capitalist world—and also in the political conflicts that led to its demise in 1876.

Marx is perhaps best known for his argument that the history of human society was, at root, the history of class struggle, and that this struggle (fueled by the contradictions intrinsic to the pre-vailing economic and social order) must necessarily culminate in a working-class revolution that would ultimately bring about the end of class-divided society and enable all humans to realize their full potential. Marx's theoretical writings such as his three-volume *Capital* and *The German Ideology* (the latter, like much of his work, published after his death) were taken up by a new generation as the socialist movement entered the main currents of political debate in the early twentieth century. Marx's ideas remain central to econom-ic, philosophical, and political analysis today. But as his ideas have been more widely taken up, they have also been recast in ways often difficult to reconcile with Marx's own approach.

While Marx is often characterized as a rather vulgar materialist, he always placed great emphasis upon the importance of ideas. In an 1842 article in his newspaper, he wrote that "practical attempts, even mass attempts, can be answered by cannon as soon as they be-come dangerous, whereas ideas . . . to which reason has fettered our conscience, are chains from which one cannot free oneself without a broken heart" (*Marx/Engels Collected Works*, vol. 1, 220–21).

And it was upon the terrain of ideas that Marx took up his strug-gle. Marx served the German radical cause as a journalist. While Marx's contemporary and rival Mikhail Bakunin rushed from bar-ricade to barricade as Europe was convulsed by rebellions, spending much of his life in prison as a result, Marx issued pamphlets and manifestos from exile during the events, and analyses afterwards. While critiquing those for whom philosophy and history were mere efforts to interpret the world—the point, he insisted, was to transform it—Marx focused his efforts on developing and disseminating a radical critique that could foreground and heighten the contradictions intrinsic to modern society and inform the nascent socialist movement in its struggles. Although Marx did not believe ideas or determination alone could transform society—men make history, he famously remarked, but not in conditions of their own choosing—he was convinced that much of Europe had reached a stage where capitalism was pushing against its limits, and the possibility of working-class revolution loomed on the horizon.

It is impossible in so short a survey to do justice to Marx's ideas. His collected works run to fifty volumes. Those volumes include works on economics, history, philosophy, politics, and revolutionary struggle, written over the course of more than forty years during which his ideas and emphases continued to evolve. While much of his later efforts were focused on his analysis of capitalism and its economics, even *Capital* is infused with the philosophical musings about human nature and alienation that dominated his earlier (and unpublished until 1932) *Economic and Philosophical Manuscripts*. Since Marx's death, thousands of scholars have devoted their careers to explicating and further developing his ideas in a wide range of disciplines.

Marx wrote little directly addressing questions of ethics or moral philosophy, proclaiming that he sought to understand the world as it was, not as it ought to be. And yet a clear outrage against alienation and exploitation is present throughout much of his work, and Marx discusses workers' dehumanization under capitalism in terms that are not only richly descriptive but also implicitly value-driven. To this dehumanization, Marx counterposed an ethical vision of a society based upon human dignity—a society in which labor becomes free because it is carried out by conscious participants in a community given over to cooperation and the pursuit of commonly agreed-upon aims. It is in the process of participation, of sharing in the decision making and direction of the communal productive and social spheres, that human beings realize their potential as self-directed, free social beings.

For Marx, the fundamental issue facing society was alienation. Human beings, through their collective activity, created and maintained human consciousness, social organization, and wealth, but had become alienated—separated from—what were not only the fruits of their labor but also the preconditions for the realization of their full human capacity. The items that human labor produces—whether ideas or automobiles—are produced at another's direction, under conditions not of the worker's choosing, for purposes that the worker does not control, and ultimately belong not to those who produce them but rather to the owners of industry. Even the capacity to labor is under the control of others; indeed, the products that workers produced in the past often enable the owners to dispense with labor in the present—just as cable television networks endlessly recycle earlier programs rather than hire actors, writers, and camera crews to produce new ones.

It is because of this alienation, Marx argued, that humanity experiences its labor as an unpleasant necessity, rather than an opportunity for self-actualization and freedom. "The worker therefore only feels himself outside his work, and in his work feels outside himself. . . . His labor is therefore not voluntary, but coerced" (Struik 1964, 110–11). Given that Marx sees labor as not just necessary to meet our material needs but fundamental to what makes us human, this alienation separates the worker from not only the means of maintaining his or her immediate physical existence but also the essence of the human condition.

Marx rejected the notion central to much political philosophy that there was an intrinsic conflict between individual freedom and the needs of the broader community. Quite the contrary, man is in his essence a social being: "Just as society itself produced man as man, so is society produced by him. Activity and mind, both in their content and in the mode of existence, are social." Not only language and culture, but our very existence and the material conditions that enable us to survive, are manifestations of social activity. "The social entity . . . is no abstract universal power opposed to the single individual, but is the essential nature of each individual, . . . produced directly by their life activity" (*Marx/Engels Collected Works,* vol. 3, 217). At the same time, Marx argued against those who would subordinate the rights of the individual to the perceived interests of the broader society, noting that this misunderstood the actual relationship between men and the society they had created (instead presenting society as an alien power over them) and in practice did not serve the interests either of individuals or of the broader society they constituted.

Similarly, Marx rejected a division of labor in which some toiled at mindless labor while others directed that labor or engaged in creative activity, instead advocating a society in which people could pursue their varied interests and activities, "mak[ing] it possible for me to do one thing today and another tomorrow, to hunt in the morning, fish in the afternoon, . . . [and] criticize after dinner, just as I have a mind, without ever becoming hunter, fisherman, shepherd or critic" (Tucker 1978, 160). The reduction of people's productive activity to a handful of repetitive tasks, and in particular the separation of mental and physical labor, might yield economic gains in the short term, but at the heavy price of stunting people's ability for self-actualization.

Marx discussed communication and the creative arts within this context. For Marx, journalism—communication more generally— was central to our humanity. Historically, he wrote, learned men had "interposed themselves between the people and the mind, between life and science, between freedom and mankind."[1] But if the press was an aspect of the realization of human freedom, there could be no basis for dividing the world into those authorized to write and those not.

Himself a frequent victim of the practice in his years as a working journalist, Marx was a consistent opponent of censorship, and demanded full freedom of conscience and expression. Similarly, if, as Marx argued, communication arises out of our essential humanity, then it must not be prostituted to commercial dominance. "The writer, of course, must earn in order to be able to live and write, but he must by no means live and write to earn. . . . The primary freedom of the press lies in not being a trade. The writer who degrades the press into being a material means deserves as punishment for this internal unfreedom the external unfreedom of censorship" (*Marx/ Engels Collected Works*, vol. 1, 174–75).

This has implications that go well beyond the increasing commodification of information and culture that we are currently experiencing, seen in the consolidation of media outlets into fewer and fewer hands, the encroachment of advertising and paid product placement into newscasts and newspaper front pages, and the like, but also in cutbacks to public libraries and the migration of information from print where it is available for repeated free use to digitized information systems that sell access on a pay-per-use basis. In arguing that the reintegration of mental and manual labor is essential to realize

1. Karl Marx, "On Freedom of the Press," chap. 6. http://www.marxists.org/archive/ marx/works/1842/free-press/ch06.html.

our full humanity, Marx implicitly challenges the division between professional communicators and audiences, a division that necessarily relegates the vast majority to passivity. And the professionalization of communication itself—a fairly recent process in which communicators no longer wield their pens on behalf of causes in which they are deeply engaged, but instead craft and disseminate ideas not their own and produce media artifacts in accordance with external criteria that leave little room for personal commitments and often require journalists to incorporate statements they know to be misleading—is itself a clear example of the alienation that Marx deplored.

Note on sources: Marx's works are available in several editions and translations, including the *Collected Works* issued by International Publishers and held by most research libraries, and in a number of anthologies. The Marxists Internet Archive (www.marxists.org) includes works by Marx and hundreds of other thinkers (mostly) in the socialist tradition(s) in several languages.

■   ■   ■

Kamenka, Eugene. 1972. *Ethical Foundations of Marxism.* 2nd ed. London: Routledge and Kegan Paul.

Marx, Karl, and Friedrich Engels. 1975–2005. *Marx/Engels Collected Works.* Moscow: Progress Publishers. Jointly issued by Lawrence and Wishart and International Publishers.

Struik, Dirk, ed. 1964. *The Economic and Philosophical Manuscripts of 1844.* New York: International Publishers.

Tucker, Robert, ed. 1978. *The Marx-Engels Reader.* 2nd ed. New York: W. W. Norton and Company.

26

John Dewey
Democratic Conversation

LEE WILKINS

Philosopher John Dewey was an intellectual child of the Enlightenment tempered by a young adulthood in an America experimenting with reform. The result was a wide-ranging philosophical vision of which ethics was a central, but by no means solitary, part. To summarize Dewey is to invite reductionism, but his approach to ethics could be characterized as follows: individual ethical choice arises from the community in which the individual finds himself. Choice must be evaluated from multiple perspectives and is always concerned with the impact on the democratic community of which the individual is an organic part. Journalism played a significant role in Dewey's vision.

Dewey was born in Burlington, Vermont, on October 20, 1859, the third of four sons born to Archibald and Lucina Dewey. Although his family had a farming heritage, his father moved to town to establish a grocery business. Biographers described Dewey as a shy, self-effacing young man, a quality he carried with him into adulthood. His mother was more ambitious for her children than his father, but both were inspired by their evangelical Protestant faith, an approach that influenced Dewey's thought although he abandoned formal religion as an adult.

Dewey came to intellectual maturity at a time of worldwide intellectual ferment; the rationality of the Enlightenment was giving way to the insights of Freud, Darwin had reoriented humanity's relation to the natural world, and the insights of Einstein, although several years in the future, were to fundamentally reshape the physical world. Dewey had access to all of these changes through his favorite reading, British publications such as the *Contemporary Review,* the *Nineteenth Century* and the *Fortnightly Review.* Closer to home, he was influenced by the beginning of the Progressive movement in the United States. Progressivism, which became nationally influential during the first decade of the twentieth century, asserted that smart government was good government and that the focus of both was human improvement and well-being. From these intellectual foundations, Dewey developed the concept of the continuing social experiment—which is how Dewey characterized democratic life—and his view that the results of the experiment, particularly social policy, must be evaluated rationally in a scientific way. This process, Dewey believed, would provide feedback to the public. Citizens would, in turn, make political choices to move the social experiment forward.

Dewey's theory of truth, which is essential to understanding the rest of his philosophy, had as its primary purpose "to show that the methods by which truth is won in the sciences are more important than any single result."[1] Dewey's belief in the scientific method was undoubtedly influenced by the university at which he earned his doctorate, Johns Hopkins, which was the U.S. institution most devoted to advancing knowledge through scientific inquiry. Just as it does today, logic and empiricism provided the dominant intellectual framework at Hopkins, a legacy of Enlightenment thinking critical to Dewey's philosophical approach.

While some biographers attribute Dewey's lifelong fascination with the impact of community on human progress to his New England childhood, Robert Westbrook, in his authoritative study, suggests that Dewey's first wife, Alice, had at least as much to do with his progressive turn of mind. Alice Dewey was an extraordinary woman whose grandfather was an adopted member of the Chippewa Indian tribe. From him, Alice inherited a disdain for social conventions and a critical social conscience. Dewey credited her with a keen intelligence and social concern, saying that it was she who had put the "guts and stuffing" into his often abstract, intellectual work. Alice was known to lecture family and friends on the importance of writers such as Emile Zola, whose work on the European continent (for example, the novel *Germinal*) foreshadowed efforts by journalists such as Upton Sinclair, who combined in-person reporting with literary device (*The Jungle, The Brass Check*) to prod the political system toward social justice.

1. S. Hook, *John Dewey: An Intellectual Portrait,* 87.

Dewey's fascination with journalism and its role in a democracy also began early in his career. His initial foray, "The Thought News," never saw the light of day. In 1890 Dewey wanted to spread his ideas beyond the classroom and had his first of several encounters with eccentric journalist Franklin Ford. Ford had quit his New York newspaper job to found a national "sociological newspaper" that would focus on the reporting of social trends, replacing the sort of scattershot, event-oriented journalism of the day. Dewey signed on, in the belief that such a publication would promote social justice and that the beginnings of such a movement "rested on the ability of individuals to become conscious of their 'function' in an interdependent community. Consciousness is social in so far as any individual consciously directs his own activities in view of the social relations involved."[2] Thus, the newspaper's mission would be to redistribute knowledge. Ford announced the new publication, which would circulate in southern Michigan, only to have the concept savagely lampooned in the local media. No such newspaper ever appeared, although Dewey said that his goal in supporting the effort had not been to change journalism but to breathe new life into philosophy.

However, that work also could be done in the classroom, and in 1894 Dewey accepted the chairmanship of the Department of Philosophy and Pedagogy at the University of Chicago. As was typical at that time, the philosophy department included the disciplines of psychology and philosophy. At Chicago, Dewey became one of the founders of the school of functionalist psychology, an approach methodologically tied to experiments with observable phenomena. Dewey's biographers and critics note that his understanding of experimental psychology and theory building was somewhat suspect; however, the whole notion of an experiment that has an impact on the subjects' responses was to characterize Dewey's thought from this point onward.

As the nature of his administrative duties suggested, Dewey also was faced with a second problem—how to develop a "science" of ethics that employed the scientific method as a way to reveal ethical knowledge.

If scientists were to apply the genetic method to ethics, eventually the trail would lead back to some protohuman "missing

2. Robert B. Westbrook, *John Dewey and American Democracy*, 53.

link"—with the following result: If, for example, the earlier stage shows only social instincts on the part of the animal, then, somehow or other, the later manifestations of human conscience are only animal instincts disguised and overlaid.[3]

Dewey's defense of this view, published first in "The Evolutionary Method as Applied to Morality," raised at least as many questions as it answered. He continued to believe in rational agency, and he continued to maintain that scientists could study human qualities such as character, dispositions, habits, emotions, and desires using the same methods as the natural sciences with a shared goal: getting at the nature of the human experience.[4] As Dewey noted in his introduction to ethics, published in 1908, "If we can discover [scientific] ethical principles, these ought to give some guidance for the unsolved problems of life which continually present themselves for decision. Whatever may be true for other sciences, it would seem that ethics at least ought to have some practical value."[5]

The appointment at Chicago was significant for another reason: it introduced Dewey to contemporary scholarship and debates in education. If there is an American thinker who set the standard and approach for education in the twentieth century, from defined curricula to various methods of evaluation, it is Dewey. Indeed, it is difficult to overstate his contributions to that field.

As an intellect, Dewey needed to find some way to connect, with additional explanatory power, this wide range of applied work with its deeply philosophical genesis. This spawned the philosophical movement of Pragmatism, and most consider Dewey one of its founders. Pragmatism can, at some level, be understood through a reference to its opposite: idealism. Pragmatists believe that, instead of reality and human thought reflecting a single idea, differing realities—shaped by historical and individual experience—define how human beings think. Dewey called what human beings think "knowledge" and argued that experience shaped it. Hence knowledge did not constitute a singular "entity" but rather was framed by experiences that could differ radically among people and groups. This pragmatic turn of mind, the notion that reality can vary depending on who is doing the perceiving, is one foundational assumption of critical and cultural

3. J. Welchman, *Dewey's Ethical Thought*, 133.
4. Ibid., 145.
5. Ibid., 176.

studies. It also helps explain many research findings, for example, that different people can hear the same message but interpret it quite differently. Pragmatism assumes an active audience, and the issue of how to grab and hold an active audience is the driving concern for both advertising practitioners and journalists today. For Dewey, pragmatism was an American philosophy, rooted in the practical concerns of how democracies grow and change in response to circumstance. How these changes could be rationally evaluated and shaped by continuing social and political experiments led Dewey intellectually to his discussion of democracy and the public's role in democratic governance.

Dewey believed that democracy was a continuing experiment and that the democratic state was "something to be scrutinized, investigated and searched for. Almost as soon as its form is stabilized, it needs to be re-made." Dewey theorized an expansive role for the democratic state, one that could be active in private associations as well as public policy; he believed that community extended beyond political associations. However, he also said "only through constant watchfulness and criticism of public officials by citizens can a state be animated in integrity and usefulness."[6] Here, clearly, was a role for journalism and for news of the day—particularly the muckrakers and their contemporary offspring, investigative reporters.

Dewey was less clear about how the public should organize itself. At several places, he seemed to equate the public with what Rousseau, about 150 years earlier, had called "the general will." "There can be no public without full publicity in respect to all consequences which concern it" (Dewey 1954, 167). At other times, Dewey used the term "the public interest," by which he appeared to mean a collection of smaller publics, each concerned with subsets of the public policy agenda. This lack of specificity has maddened generations of political philosophers who have noted that Dewey's insistence that organizing a democracy is a purely "intellectual" problem has created all sorts of mischief when applying his theory to real political life. All agree that Dewey placed community first, arguing that the community took primacy over any institutional, governmental organization; an enlightened public took precedence over even enlightened governmental administrators. Further, community was geographic—place mattered.

6. Westbrook, *Dewey and Democracy,* 303, 305.

Enlivening that community was the specific work of analytic and public policy–oriented journalism, which Dewey said would "have such an enormous and widespread human bearing that its bare existence would be an irresistible invitation to a presentation of it which would have a direct popular appeal . . . Consequently, the 'freeing of the artist in literary presentation' was as much a condition of the creation of an effective public as the freeing of social inquiry."[7] Dewey's call for this sort of journalism has been seconded by scholars such as Kathleen Hall Jamieson, who argue that political journalists need a different definition of news, one that deemphasizes polarized conflict and focuses instead on multiple solutions to public policy questions. This approach would change political journalism profoundly. It is not a stretch to suggest that Dewey's conceptualization of an involved public also gives philosophical weight to movements such as citizen journalism, which takes the collection and reporting of facts out of the hands of the professionals and places the work of constructing "knowledge" (as Dewey used the term) in the hands of citizens. Dewey believed public policy was best formulated by an informed citizenry, although he agreed with Walter Lippmann that such a "public mind" did not yet exist. But, it was only at the local, community level that Dewey believed the chance of forming such a public mind—through organic connection to a geographic community—could be encouraged.

> Systematic and continuous inquiry into all the conditions which affect association and their dissemination in print is a precondition of the creation of a true public. But it and its results are but tools after all. Their final actuality is accomplished in face-to-face relationships by means of direct give and take. . . . Ideas which are not communicated, shared and reborn in expression are but soliloquy, and soliloquy is but broken and imperfect thought. (Dewey 1954, 218)

Dewey's political thought, and hence his conceptualization of a role for journalism, must be placed in the larger context of his philosophy to be understood. Dewey believed the democratic experiment would move the country toward a society where social justice was the predominant value. His pragmatic understanding of the truth meant

---

7. Ibid., 311.

that Dewey believed the different publics that constitute society would need to negotiate extant political arrangements—continually. His belief in education as a way to inform that end—and journalism's role as the linchpin of that educational effort—is unequaled in contemporary philosophy. The fact that Dewey considered such journalism the equal of literary artistry has been generally ignored, although journalists, in their secret hearts, view themselves as almost equal parts craftspeople, social scientists, and artists.

Dewey's formulation of this change-agent journalistic role is the core understanding of communitarian theory as applied to media ethics. His work contains insights about political communication, how it is both constructed and understood, that carry weight today. And, his effort to link practical ethics to deeply philosophical questions, for example whether there can be a science of ethics housed and understood within the human mind, forecasts work that is emerging only now, more than one hundred years after Dewey first articulated the issue. In all these areas, Dewey's thought remains provocative. In his willingness to connect journalism to the maintenance of a democratic community, his thinking provides journalists with both aspiration and some intriguing suggestions for daily practice.

■　■　■

Dewey, John. 1954. *The Public and Its Problems.* Chicago: Swallow Press.

Hook, S. 1995. *John Dewey: An Intellectual Portrait.* New York: Prometheus Publications.

Welchman, J. 1995. *Dewey's Ethical Thought.* Ithaca, N.Y.: Cornell University Press.

Westbrook, Robert B. 1991. *John Dewey and American Democracy.* Ithaca, N.Y.: Cornell University Press.

27

Jürgen Habermas
Consensus and Citizenship

DAVID S. ALLEN

The political implications of the work of Jürgen Habermas have been widely examined, especially his desire to cling to the potential of consensus. There is little doubt that Habermas's desire to retain connection with Enlightenment thought and the possibility of consensus is one of the most controversial parts of his work. Some see Habermas's belief in the possibility of consensus as naive if not impossible, while others argue that it is discourse itself that is at the center of democracy rather than consensus. However, commentators are beginning to realize that for Habermas consensus plays a much more complicated role than originally thought. Consensus is not simply an anticipated goal or end product central to political decision-making. Rather, consensus also has an ethical component that tells us something about what it means to be a citizen in a democratic society. It reflects an attitude that citizens bring to the discourse and as such points us to the responsibilities of citizenship. In important ways, then, consensus is at the very core of what it means to be ethical citizens living in a democratic society or, as this chapter will argue, what it means to be a deliberative citizen.

Habermas was born in 1929 in Düsseldorf, Germany. From 1971 to 1983, he was the director of the Max Planck Institute in Germany. He retired from teaching in 1993 but remains an active writer. He is widely considered to be the intellectual heir to what has come to be known as the Frankfurt School of critical theory. Habermas studied under the guidance of one of the Frankfurt School's founders, Theodor Adorno. As early as 1969, he was recognized as one of the leading German social theorists. However, it was not until the publication of the

English translation of his book *The Structural Transformation of the Public Sphere* in 1989 that he achieved similar standing in the United States and North America. His writings cover a wide variety of topics, including a history of public opinion and media, a critique of science, a theory of social interaction, the formulation of what has come to be called discourse or communicative ethics, and, most recently, a broad-based theory of democracy based on the idea of discourse. His works synthesize a diverse range of thinkers and reconstruct their ideas in new ways. And one of his important achievements is making deliberation central to democratic life.

How Habermas has done that is often lost in the complex nature of his work. Carol Gould in her *Rethinking Democracy* (1988) has criticized him for not putting forward a theory of democracy, but rather a theory of social interaction. That criticism seems particularly justified when looking at segments of his work, especially his later, more theoretical work. But if his work is considered as a whole, the link to democracy and citizenship becomes evident.

At the foundation of Habermas's critical theory of society is his view of how individuals relate to society. Building on the ideas of Emile Durkheim and George Herbert Mead, Habermas puts forward a picture of society where community is primary—a view of society where individualism is created through and by society. As Habermas in his *Theory of Communicative Action* puts it: "How can we at one and the same time belong wholly to ourselves and just as completely to others." Whereas Durkheim saw morality beginning with membership in a group, Mead recognized that culture was transmitted through communication in language. Habermas argues that Mead's essential point was that meaning can be traced to the community. As he notes, "Meaning is a systemic property . . . meanings are constituted in species-specific environments, they are not at the disposition of the individual exemplar as such" (*Theory*, 7). Habermas's use of Mead breaks with traditional liberal thought, preferring to base democracy on its discursive framework rather than on individual rights and freedom.

Building on that view of how society is comprised, Habermas sees the purpose of what he calls communicative action not in obtaining success in an argument, but rather as a way of reaching understanding. This emphasis leads Habermas to speech act theory. Habermas builds on the idea that every speech act has a propositional and performative aspect. Habermas argues that inherent in any speech act is the recognition or acknowledgment that the two sides can come to an understanding or agreement. He argues that unless two sides have that basic understanding, conversation would not take place—there would be no reason for people to enter into a discussion. But perhaps more importantly, Habermas believes he can link reason with communication. In speech, Habermas contends, is the understanding that through the logic of the best argument, consensus will be reached. Habermas writes in *The Theory of Communicative Action:*

> The term "reaching understanding" means, at the minimum, that at least two speaking and acting subjects understand a linguistic expression in the same way. The meaning of an elementary expression consists in the contribution that it makes to the meaning of an acceptable speech act. (307)

For Habermas, deliberative citizenship is built on the notion that people enter discourse with a desire to use reason to attain a consensus in order to live in a democratic society. But how is that consensus achieved and what role does it play in ethical, deliberative citizenship? Part of the answer to that question lies in how citizens ought to interact with each other. And while Habermas seldom uses the term, the idea of transparency is central to this project.

Habermas's work is an attempt to address the institutional weaknesses of Kantian Enlightenment philosophy while overcoming the Hegelian critique that centers on the twin notions of publicity and participation. Hegel called into question Kant's desire to evaluate institutions and their practices in isolation from each other, arguing that institutions were interrelated.[1] Habermas sought to overcome this concern by emphasizing citizen participation and the transparency of public life. Publicity is a way of achieving transparency, and transparency aids participation by allowing citizens to share their beliefs and ideals, which allows people to realize commonalities with others in society.

Transparency is central to Habermas's project at many stages. In *The Structural Transformation of the Public Sphere* (1989), he noted the importance of transparency for public institutions, especially political parties and the press. Calling the press the public sphere's pre-

---

1. Seyla Benhabib, *Critique, Norm, and Utopia: A Study of the Foundations of Critical Theory*, 76–77.

eminent institution, he also noted how professionalization changed the press.[2] Habermas called not only for the inner workings of these institutions to be made public, but also asked that the linkages between the institutions be made transparent. As he wrote: "This would include, for instance, requiring that the organizations provide the public with information concerning the source and deployment of their financial means" (*Structural Transformation*, 209). Even in this early work, however, Habermas noted the dangers inherent in publicity, detailing how staged political events work against the realization of a properly functioning public sphere (210–11).

How the notion of transparency underlies his entire discourse theory of democracy was identified in Habermas's later work. It is fundamental to what Habermas terms universal pragmatics, the very notion so central to discourse between citizens. In its simplest form, universal pragmatics refers to the assumptions made by citizens when they engage in discourse. Universal pragmatics refers to the notion that when people enter into a discourse, they do so based on the assumption that speakers will try to communicate clearly and that they will tell the truth. Without that assumption, it would be impossible, in Habermas's mind, for citizens to achieve understanding, the goal of all properly situated discourse.

Habermas's belief in the ability of people to reach understanding through communication is at the heart of two ideas that remain central to his project: the ideal speech situation and discourse ethics. The ideal speech situation is for Habermas more or less taken for granted in the domain of discourse. As Thomas McCarthy explains, it is a goal that speakers seldom achieve, but an assumption that is made "whenever we enter into discourse with the intention of arriving at rational agreement about truth claims."[3]

Closely related to the ideal speech situation is Habermas's idea of discourse ethics. It is here that moral principles serve as a guide for interpreters and actors engaged in practical discourse. More importantly, it is through this discourse guided by these ethical standards that citizens go about turning particular (individual) interests into generalizable (universal) interests. Transparency is central to that

---

2. See David Allen, "Defining a Professional Mission: The Law and the Question of Public Representation," 82–102.

3. Thomas McCarthy, *The Critical Theory of Jürgen Habermas*, 309.

transformation, as Habermas writes in his essay, "A Reply to My Critics": "(I)f the actors do not bring with them, and into their discourse, *their* individual life-histories, *their* identities, *their* needs and wants, *their* traditions, membership and so forth, practical discourse would at once be robbed of all content" (255). The transformation of particular interests to generalizable interests follows the rules of discourse ethics. In short, a norm can only be considered to be valid if all who would be affected have consented to it, after considering potential consequences and side effects, and if it is valid universally.

Transparency, then, is central to Habermas's project at many levels. It requires participants in discourse to be transparent so that some understanding can be achieved. And more importantly for Habermas, it is in the transparent nature of dialogue that he is able to avoid Hegel's critique of Kantian ethics. It is through the dialogic nature of his ethics, and the idea of transparency that grounds the dialogue, that he is able to avoid problems encountered by Kant.

Consensus, as can be seen, plays a far more complicated role in Habermasian thought than the simple notion that citizens can reach agreement on how to live their lives. Universal pragmatics, the ideal speech situation, discourse ethics, and the notion of transparency are all central building blocks in the notion of consensus. Consensus presupposes that citizens can reach mutual consent on controversial issues through deliberation not because of some naive idealism, but rather because it points us to the ethic that ought to guide our interactions with other citizens.

For Habermas, this notion of mutual consent is both a factor in the characters of citizens and in the moral development of citizens. The value of consensus is not simply that we can and might be able to come to some agreement on what we ought to do, but that the search for consensus allows us to understand the other, guides our search for understanding, and shapes how we ought to treat people with whom we might disagree. For Habermas, then, the idea of consensus is important because it influences how we interact with others. When a person agrees to enter into a conversation with another person, the understanding is that we will treat each other with respect, and be open to the search for understanding. If those assumptions do not exist, Habermas argues, there is little reason to enter into the discourse. The important, two-prong influence of consensus is captured by Habermas in *Moral Consciousness and Communicative Action:*

> Without the individual's uninfringeable freedom to respond with a "yes" or "no" to criticizable validity claims, consent is merely factual rather than truly universal. Conversely, without empathetic sensitivity by each person to everyone else, no solution deserving universal consent will result from the deliberation. These two aspects—the autonomy of inalienable individuals and their embeddedness in an intersubjectively shared web of relations—are internally connected, and it is this link that the procedure of discursive decision making takes into account. (202)

Habermas's notion of consensus is important far beyond its theoretical boundaries. It is increasingly relevant as we negotiate today's mediated world. Whether consensus is achievable is really less the issue. More important is that Habermas's ethical theory guides us to approach citizenship in a different way. It is a citizenship that is less focused on winning an argument or political victory and more about trying to understand the position of others. In fact, it requires us to deal with the "other" as rational beings entitled to respect and equality.

Today's political world is dominated by what Habermas would call strategic communication—communication that is aimed at achieving dominance rather than understanding. It is reflected in political dialogue, advertising, public relations, entertainment programming, and often in our day-to-day interactions with others. It is important to note that this form of strategic communication is not simply associated with left or right, profit or nonprofit, but permeates all of society at a very deep level. The result of this domination is that rational discussion of important moral issues is frequently avoided within today's society. Amy Gutmann and Dennis Thompson have argued in their book *Why Deliberative Democracy?* that the belief by citizens that a consensus cannot be reached has led to decisions to remove moral discussion from the agenda. Citizens look for legal or procedural answers instead of dealing with difficult moral questions. The critical problem for Gutmann and Thompson is how we deal with resolving those moral conflicts.[4]

Habermas's work provides a starting point to address that problem. It requires us to recognize the dominance of the perspective that encourages us to avoid difficult moral issues and to do all we can to

---

4. Amy Gutmann and Dennis Thompson, *Why Deliberative Democracy?* 78.

change how we interact with others, both as citizens and institutions. While Habermas's ethical theory points the way to significant political/institutional reform, at its core is an often overlooked call for citizens to approach public life in a vastly different way. Democracy, in the end, ought to be less about domination and winning and more about the search for consensus and understanding that is central to deliberative citizenship.

■ ■ ■

Allen, David S. 2005. "Defining a Professional Mission: The Law and the Question of Public Representation." In *Democracy, Inc.: The Press and Law in the Corporate Rationalization of the Public Sphere* (Urbana: University of Illinois Press), 82–102.

Benhabib, Seyla. 1986. *Critique, Norm, and Utopia: A Study of the Foundations of Critical Theory.* New York: Columbia University Press.

Gould, Carol C. 1988. *Rethinking Democracy.* Cambridge, UK: Cambridge University Press.

Gutmann, Amy, and Dennis Thompson. 2004. *Why Deliberative Democracy?* Princeton, N.J.: Princeton University Press.

Habermas, Jürgen. 1981, 1989. *The Theory of Communicative Action.* 2 vols. Translated by Thomas McCarthy. Boston: Beacon Press.

———. 1982. "A Reply to My Critics." In John B. Thompson and David Held, eds., *Habermas: Critical Debates* (Cambridge, Mass.: MIT Press), 219–83.

———. 1989. *The Structural Transformation of the Public Sphere: An Inquiry into a Category of Bourgeois Society.* Translated by Thomas Burger and Fredrick Lawrence. Cambridge, Mass.: MIT Press.

———. 1990. *Moral Consciousness and Communicative Action.* Translated by Christian Lenhardt and Shierry Weber Nicholsen. Cambridge, Mass.: MIT Press.

McCarthy, Thomas. 1988. *The Critical Theory of Jürgen Habermas.* Cambridge, Mass.: MIT Press.

28

Emmanuel Levinas
Priority of the Other

RONALD C. ARNETT

This introductory treatment of Emmanuel Levinas's ethics project for the field of communication begins with three basic assumptions. First, Levinas brings ethics to the very center of life as an ongoing continuing act of creation. Second, Levinas's understanding of communication begins with listening, not with telling. Third, listening connects the person to this primordial ethical echo, an echo that is a priori to oneself and the empirical person before us. Levinas offers a fundamental critique of humanism, asserting that it misses the phenomenological nature of human existence.

The power of Levinas's project manifests itself in its ability to disturb, to claim our attention. He asks us to recant the blasphemy so that we can build a "better" self, offering instead the reminder to listen to an ethical echo that calls out a "better" self. His project attends to an ethical echo that was and will be there, forever linked to human existence. This ethical call turns us toward the face of the Other that moves us toward an accompanying attentive response.

To outline Levinas's contribution to communication, the following sections illuminate the "who," the "what," and the "why" of his contribution: 1) a brief biography of Emmanuel Levinas, 2) the major concepts of Levinas's project, and 3) a suggestion about the ongoing importance of Levinas for the study and practice of human communication. Like Dietrich Bonhoeffer, Levinas lived in a time of Nazi tyranny. Where Bonhoeffer pointed toward "a world come of age" that calls forth the responsibility of a person of religious conviction, Levinas reminds us to listen to an ethical echo that points us toward responsibility for the Other.

Levinas, as a Jewish philosopher deeply knowledgeable about the Talmud and, additionally, a primary expert on and critic of the work of Martin Heidegger, shook the foundations of conventional Western philosophy, bringing forth an understanding of communicative life that suggests that "modern" ethics and the "modern" understanding of communication have met a moral cul de sac. His project is a prophetic call to rectify our understanding of what it means to be at home with one another. His message is profound, troubling, and provocative. I cannot totally accept the insights of Levinas. His ideas are not easy to accept and even more difficult to dismiss. Yet, I repeatedly return to his project, which is, itself, an ethical echo, persistently calling us to listen to an a priori chant, "I am my brother's keeper," that shapes existence prior to the first act of human beings attempting to shape themselves.

Who: Emmanuel Levinas

Emmanuel Levinas was born in 1905 in Kaunas, Lithuania. He died in 1995. In 1930, he became a naturalized French citizen. Levinas's education was philosophical from the beginning; he studied and befriended some of the best minds in Europe. In 1923, he started his formal study of philosophy at Strasbourg University; during that time, his friendship with Maurice Blanchot began. Blanchot's work influenced Levinas and Diderot; Blanchot's emphasis upon paradox and early poststructuralistic writing were significant insights. Additionally, Blanchot's friendship assisted Levinas's family most profoundly; he saved the life of Levinas's wife and daughter during the Holocaust.

In 1928, Levinas attended Freiburg University to study with the leading figure in phenomenology, Edmund Husserl. Of course, at Freiburg, Levinas met Husserl's former student and emerging idea extender and contender, Martin Heidegger, whose *Being and Time* (1962) brought forth the power of an existential-phenomenological position and had a significant impact on Levinas's work for the remainder of his life. Levinas both admired Heidegger's work and considered it misguided; Levinas considered ethics, not Being, as the foundation of human existence. Levinas had a similar view of Heidegger himself, admiring him while simultaneously being angered by his support of National Socialism.

In the German invasion of France in 1940, Levinas joined the French military, only to have his unit captured quickly. He spent the remainder of the war in a prison camp, not a concentration camp, due to the third Geneva Convention which stated that prisoners of war must remain in a prison camp. During that time, and at great personal risk, Maurice Blanchot assisted Levinas's wife and daughter, finding them sanctuary during the war in a monastery. They were the only members of the Levinas family spared from the Holocaust; Levinas never saw his mother-in-law, father, or brothers again. During his imprisonment, Levinas kept copious notes, which later led to two works: *De l'Existence à l'Existent* (1978) and *Le Temps et l'Autre* (1979).

Levinas had numerous powerful philosophical influences prior to the war, including the two major figures of phenomenology and existential phenomenology, Husserl and Heidegger, respectively. Levinas's early scholarship centered primarily on phenomenology with foreshadowing of his later project on ethics as first philosophy. It was during the war that Levinas began to come into his own, beginning with his original work on ethics that offered an alternative to the West and a contending voice to Heidegger. He outlined ethics as prior to the question of Being. Levinas's first major work was *Totality and Infinity* (1961), emerging in response to Heidegger, Franz Rosenzweig, and Martin Buber. He framed dialogic encounters differently than other major scholars, moving face-to-face interaction out of the realm of reciprocity and into the realm of the ethical. Levinas's second major work was *Otherwise than Being or Beyond Essence* (1974), which contended with Heidegger most directly and influenced the work of many, including Jacques Derrida.

Levinas's commitment to understand life as "otherwise than Being" led him to engage language differently than convention, interrogating language, deconstructing and disrupting the use and significance of both philosophical terminology and everyday vocabulary. He rejected reification of his work and spurned efforts to invite undue confidence in any set or rigid system of ideas. Again, moving otherwise from Western convention, Levinas did not seek to underscore the "sameness" of phenomena, but to attend to their difference. The alterity of the Other, the radical difference of the Other, drove the heart of his project. From the beginning moments of philosophical study with two of the best minds in the West to becoming a witness to the ongoing failure of the West in Nazi hands, Levinas sketched for us what he heard, an ethical echo that begins not within a cave, but upon the *visage de l'autre.*

What: The Ideas

The philosophy of ethics that Levinas proposes cannot find its way into a formula or format; he worked deliberately at not reifying his project. Thus, the following effort to provide a handle on his work begins with admission of limits. One can point to the ongoing Levinas project in the following fashion: 1) the origin of human existence rests with an ethical echo; 2) the face of the Other reminds us of that echo; 3) we are held hostage by our obligation to the Other, an obligation informed by an earlier voice (an ethical echo); 4) the face of the Other is an ethical signpost that shifts us from sight to phenomenological listening.

1. *An ethical echo* began long before we stepped upon this planet. The echo is simply, "I am my brother's keeper." Levinas supports this statement with phenomenological justification. Since we are social creatures, without the Other, there is no "I." If we do not take care of the Other, we cease to be human. What makes us human is not "me" alone, but our ability to learn from and to engage the Other. Sociability is at the heart of humanness. The ethical echo that insists upon our taking care of the Other is the originative home of humanness. The ethical echo of "I am my brother's keeper" is the music that welcomes another into a human home. One might say that to suggest that one is acting in an inhuman fashion is to place that person outside a human home. Yet, for Levinas, such a judgment is not the central point of his ethics. His question is not whether the Other is acting in a human fashion, but whether or not "I" am. Ethics for Levinas begins with listening to an ethical echo that calls one into responsibility; the focus is not upon the limits of the Other and whether the Other attends to an ethical echo.

2. *The face of the Other* is not a metaphor, but a real face. Levinas views the human face as the door to the human home of sociality. The face is a door that opens into a home filled with the echo described above. Understanding the face as a door suggests the importance of the face as an entrance—not an entrance into a given life, but entrance into a call to responsibility. A given face is a particular door that offers a unique call to responsibility without dictating its form. The directness of this ethical call is more akin to jazz than to

classical music in that there is a thematic call and the necessity for individual variation.

Levinas stated that it is important not to attend to the color of another's eyes when attending to a given face. It is not the unique person (face) that guides one's responsibility. However, the face of the Other is real, not metaphorical; the face acts as an entrance into the human home, filled with music that repeatedly chants an ethical echo that calls one to responsibility. For Levinas, the face of the Other holds us hostage.

3. *The hostage* language that Levinas employs is disturbing. He catches our attention by the fact that we do not hold another hostage, but that the Other holds us hostage. The face of the Other takes us to an ethical echo that reminds us of an obligation to another, no matter the cost. For Levinas, the guest in the dwelling or human home holds the in-dweller hostage. This demanding language manifests itself with loud clarity when one assumes responsibility for another, particularly when one is a parent. For instance, when I was a young parent, my son asked, "Dad, are you my friend, and will you always be my friend?" I looked into the eyes of my son and, without thinking of any theory or any parenting technique, said, "Yes, I am your friend, but if I had to give up your friendship to be your Dad (to be responsible for you), I would do so without hesitation. I hope to be your friend, but I will always be your Dad first and foremost. You can count on me to do what you may not like if I had to do so to help you. I would give up your friendship in an instant to be responsible as your Dad." I then left my son's room and thought of the faces that were before me in that meeting: first my son, and, second, at the end of the conversation I was attending to a phenomenological face—that of my Dad, who seemed to be talking to me as I talked to my son. My Dad seemed to say to me, "Remember that responsibility must trump being liked by another; do what you must do. It is now your turn. That which defined me now defines you." Levinas makes that moment sensible to me. He reminds us that responsibility is demanding and that we find ourselves called out by the Other. Human faces hold us hostage; this call to responsibility is a primordial sense of "why" for our communicative action.

4. *A signpost of welcome* suggests that the face is the welcome into the dwelling of the human home, a place where one hears the music of responsibility and cannot turn back. As one begins to attend to an ethical echo, one understands how burden and meaning commingle.

It is the burden we take on for others that opens the door to human meaning in our own lives.

The face is a welcome and also a warning for all that enters the human home—responsibility of the human home in turn brings burden to the communicative agent. Unlike much of communication discussion in the last fifty years, Levinas does not seek to offer us comfort. In fact, his ethical theory points in an opposing direction—to attending to the burden of the Other, holding oneself responsible.

Levinas may not "sell" easily in a society seeking self-actualization and comfort. However, in the quiet moments of our lives when we reflect on the most meaningful uses of our existence, Levinas's notions come to life: burden, responsibility, Other, and a face that called us out to responsibility by saying, "If not you then who?" Ernest Boyer, former head of the Carnegie Foundation, understood the power of the call from the Other into acts of responsibility. When he was asked the question, "What makes a great student who has come from an unprivileged educational background?" He stated: "A Mom, Dad, brother, sister, aunt, uncle, coach, teacher, rabbi/priest, who says, 'No matter what happens I am with you; you will succeed and I will help you forever.'" Out of such burden, meaning announces itself, reminding us of the power of a "responsive 'I'" shaped by the call of the Other.

Why: The Ongoing Significance of Levinas's Project

Levinas frames communication as secondary to ethics. He places ontology and philosophy as subordinate to ethics as well. He moves ethics from a dimension of philosophical and practical life to its very center. His work begins with the assumption of "ethics as first philosophy." The contribution to communication that he makes is profound in that he critiques basic Western assumptions about the origin of individual responsibility. The lasting significance of his project is rejecting the conventional construction of the "I" and offering an even more powerful "responsive 'I'."[1] The communicative agent as a "responsive 'I'" is a derivative of the call of responsibility. The phrase, "If not me, then who?" ceases to be the mark of a heroic self, but emerges

1. Ronald C. Arnett, "The Responsive 'I': Levinas's Derivative Argument." *Argumentation and Advocacy* 40, no. 1: 39–50.

in the acquiescence to a call that begins with the face of another calling one into action.

Communication becomes the doing of ethics discovered in the act of listening to an ethical echo: "I am my brother's keeper." Communication shaped by ethics calls out the "responsive I." For Levinas, heroes do not make themselves; they answer calls to take on burdens they simply cannot ignore. Perhaps that is what Levinas did for a lifetime—he took on the burden of all who failed to return from the concentration camps. He listened to an ethical echo that calls us to communicate otherwise than convention—"I am my brother's keeper."

■ ■ ■

"The Responsive 'I': Levinas's Derivative Argument." *Argumentation and Advocacy* 40, no. 1: 39–50.

Heidegger, Martin. 1962. *Being and Time.* Translated by John MacQuarrie and Edward Robinson. New York: Harper and Row.

Levinas, Emmanuel. 1969. *Totality and Infinity.* Translated by Alphonso Lingis. Pittsburgh: Duquesne University Press.

———. 1978. *De L'existence a L'existent.* Paris: J. Vrin.

———. 1979. *Le Temps et l'Autre.* Montpellier: Fata Morgana.

———. 1998. *Otherwise than Being or Beyond Essence.* Translated by Alphonso Lingis. Pittsburgh: Duquesne University Press.

Contributors

Allen, David S. Associate Professor, Department of Journalism and Mass Communication at the University of Wisconsin–Milwaukee. Coeditor of *Freeing the First Amendment: Critical Perspectives on Freedom of Expression.* His most recent book is *Democracy, Inc.: The Press and Law in the Corporate Rationalization of the Public Sphere.*

Arnett, Ronald C. Professor and Chair, the Department of Communication and Rhetorical Studies at Duquesne University. Author or coauthor of seven books. The latest is *Dialogic Confession: Bonhoeffer's Rhetoric of Responsibility for a World Come of Age.*

Babcock, William. Professor, Southern Illinois University–Carbondale. Founder, Media Ethics Division and Co-Director of the Teaching Ethics Workshop, Association for Education in Journalism and Mass Communication.

Beasley, Maurine. Professor of Journalism, The Philip Merrill College of Journalism, University of Maryland. Research interests in journalism history, especially women's portrayal and participation in journalism. Former President, Association for Education in Journalism and Mass Communication.

Bekken, Jon. Associate Professor, Department of English and Director of the Program in Communications, Albright College (Reading, Pennsylvania). Research interests in history of journalism and labor movement communication. He is coeditor of *Radical Economics and the Labor Movement* and coauthor of *The Industrial Workers of the World: Its First 100 Years.*

Christians, Clifford G. Charles H. Sandage Distinguished Professor, Research Professor of Communications, Professor of Journalism, and Professor of Media Studies at the University of Illinois, Champaign-Urbana.

Cohen-Almagor, Raphael. Formerly Director of the Center for Democratic Studies at the University of Haifa, Israel, and Woodrow Wilson Fellow in Washington, D.C. Now Professor and Chair in Politics, Department of Politics and International Studies, at the University of Hull (UK).

Craft, Stephanie. Associate Professor of Journalism Studies, University of Missouri, School of Journalism. Research interests in press practices and performance, journalism ethics, and the media and democracy. Former Chair, the Media Ethics Division, Association for Education in Journalism and Mass Communication.

Gunkel, David J. Professor, Department of Communication at Northern Illinois University. Teaches and researches interactive media, communication technology, and philosophy of technology. His latest book is *Thinking Otherwise: Philosophy, Communication, Technology.*

Hulst, Mary. Assistant Professor, Department of Homiletics, Calvin Theological Seminary. Her research interest is media ethics and her Ph.D. dissertation focused on virtue ethics in professional communicators.

Hume, Janice. Associate Professor, Department of Journalism, Grady College of Journalism and Mass Communication, University of Georgia. Author of *Obituaries in American Culture* and coauthor of *Journalism in a Culture of Grief.*

Merrill, John C. Emeritus Professor of Journalism, University of Missouri–Columbia. Listed in *Who's Who in America, Who's Who in the World, Directory of American Scholars, International Authors and Writers,* and *Dictionary of International Biography.*

Peck, Lee Anne. Assistant Professor of Journalism and Mass Communications, School of Communication, University of Northern Colorado. Her research area is media ethics; she specifically explores best practices in the teaching of ethical decision-making.

Plaisance, Patrick Lee. Associate Professor, Department of Journalism and Technical Communication, Colorado State University. Specialty areas are media sociology, media ethics, and journalistic decision-making. He is author of the textbook *Media Ethics: Key Principles for Responsible Practice* (Sage, 2008).

Siddiqi, Mohammad A. Professor of Journalism and Public Relations, and Director of the Journalism Program, Western Illinois University. He is Secretary General of the North American Association of Muslim Professionals and Scholars. His most recent book is *Islam, Muslims, and the Media*.

Ward, Stephen J. A. James E. Burgess Professor of Journalism Ethics and Director of the Center for Journalism Ethics, School of Journalism and Mass Communication, University of Wisconsin–Madison. His latest books are *The Invention of Journalism Ethics: The Path to Objectivity and Beyond* and (coedited with H.Wasserman) *Media Ethics Beyond Borders: A Global Perspective.*

Whitehouse, Virginia. Associate Professor and Chair, Department of Communication Studies, Whitworth University (Spokane). Co-Director of the Teaching Ethics Workshop, Association for Education in Journalism and Mass Communication. Fellow, Journalism Leadership in Diversity Institute.

Wilkins, Lee. Curator's Teaching Professor in Radio-Television Journalism, University of Missouri, School of Journalism. Editor, *Journal of Mass Media Ethics.* Her two most recent books (coauthor) are *The Moral Media: How Journalists Reason about Ethics* and *Handbook of Mass Media Ethics.*

Index